INSPIRING SOCCER STORIES FOR KIDS

Fun, Inspirational Facts & Stories For Young Readers

FALCON FOCUS

Soccer is more than a game; it's a language that unites the world, a battle of strategy and skill, and a dance of passion and determination. On this field, every goal scored is a dream realized, every defeat a lesson learned, and every moment played a memory etched in the hearts of fans and players alike.

Contents

Introduction

Welcome, young soccer enthusiasts, to a world filled with excitement, dreams, and the magic of soccer! *Inspiring Soccer Stories For Kids* is a treasure trove of tales that will take you on a thrilling journey through this beautiful game. This book is not just about goals, victories, and skills on the pitch; it's about the heart, determination, and spirit of some of the greatest heroes of soccer.

As you turn these pages, you will meet legendary players like Pelé, whose dazzling moves lit up the fields of Brazil, and Mia Hamm, who showed that with passion and perseverance, anything is possible. You will walk in the footsteps of Lionel Messi, feeling the joy of his childhood dreams turning into reality, and stand in the goal with Hope Solo, defending with courage and tenacity.

Each story in this book is more than just an account of matches won and goals scored. These are stories of real people who faced challenges, overcame obstacles, and followed their hearts to achieve their dreams. You will learn about their early beginnings, the challenges they faced, and the unyielding spirit that carried them through.

So, lace up your boots, get ready to cheer, and dive into these inspiring stories that celebrate the love for soccer. Whether you play the sport, are a devoted fan, or just love a good story, these tales are for you. Let's begin this adventure together and discover the magic that soccer brings to lives all around the world!

The Rise of Pelé

Early Life

Born on October 23, 1940, in Três Corações, Brazil, Edson Arantes do Nascimento, who would later be known worldwide as Pelé, began his life far from the glamour of international soccer stadiums. His family's modest background, with his father being a soccer player himself, was instrumental in shaping his early interest in the game. Pelé's father, known as Dondinho, was a professional footballer but faced a career hampered by injuries. Despite the family's financial struggles, Pelé's early life was rich in love and support, particularly for his passion for soccer.

The origin of his nickname "Pelé" is a story often recounted with a touch of humor and mystery. The name supposedly originated from his mispronunciation of the name of his favorite goalkeeper, Bile, as a child. He would often talk about the goalkeeper, but his inability to pronounce the name correctly led to his friends teasing him by calling him "Pelé," a name that had no meaning in Portuguese. Initially, he disliked the nickname, finding it too simplistic and unremarkable. Little did he know that this nickname would become a global symbol of soccer excellence.

Pelé's passion for soccer was evident from a very young age. Growing up in poverty, he couldn't afford a proper soccer ball, often playing with a sock stuffed with newspaper or a grapefruit. These humble beginnings did not deter him; instead, they fueled his imagination and honed his skills. His natural talent was evident even in these early days, as he would maneuver the makeshift ball with the same dexterity that would later dazzle the world on the soccer field.

As a young boy, Pelé took on various odd jobs to contribute to his family's income. He worked as a shoeshine boy and a waiter, but his heart always remained on the soccer field. His father became his first coach, teaching him the fundamentals of the game and nurturing his burgeoning talent. Dondinho's influence was pivotal in Pelé's development as a soccer player. He not only inherited his father's love for the game but also his skill and understanding of soccer's nuances.

In his neighborhood, Pelé would play for several amateur teams, showcasing a level of skill and understanding of the game that was extraordinary for his age. His performances in local youth leagues caught the attention of Waldemar de Brito, a former Brazilian national team player, who saw the potential in the young Pelé. De Brito took it upon himself to mentor Pelé and was instrumental in his early development as a player. He recognized that Pelé's talent was exceptional and needed a bigger stage.

Career Beginnings

At the tender age of 15, Pelé's journey into professional soccer began with Santos FC, marking the start of an era that would revolutionize the sport. His transition from playing in the streets of Três Corações to joining one of Brazil's most prestigious clubs was nothing short of a fairy tale. In 1956, under the guidance of Waldemar de Brito, Pelé arrived at Santos, a club that would become synonymous with his name.

From the outset, Pelé's talent was unmistakable. During his trial at Santos, he impressed the coaching staff with his extraordinary skill, intelligence on the field, and innate scoring ability. His performance was so compelling that he was immediately signed to the team, a decision that would change the course of the club's history. Pelé's integration into the professional sphere of soccer at such a young age was a testament to his remarkable ability and maturity.

Pelé's professional debut for Santos came on September 7, 1956, against Corinthians Santo André. The soccer world quickly took notice of this young sensation who played with the poise and creativity of a seasoned veteran. In that match, Pelé scored a goal, an early indication of the remarkable career that lay ahead. His debut was more than just a good start; it was a proclamation of his arrival on the world soccer stage.

In his first season with Santos, Pelé's impact was immediate and profound. He brought a new energy and dynamism to the team, and his style of play was both innovative and captivating. He had a unique ability to read the game, seeing opportunities where others saw none, and his ball control and shooting were already among the best in the league. Pelé finished his first professional season with an impressive tally of goals, quickly becoming a fan favorite and a key player for Santos.

The 1958 season was a turning point for both Pelé and Santos FC. At just 17 years old, Pelé led Santos to their first Campeonato Paulista championship, one of the most prestigious state championships in Brazil. He was the top scorer of the tournament, displaying a level of talent and maturity that belied his years. This achievement was a clear sign that Pelé was not just a promising young player but a force to be reckoned with in Brazilian soccer.

Pelé's successes with Santos continued to grow. He played an instrumental role in the team's domination of the Campeonato Paulista in the late 1950s and early 1960s, winning several state titles.

His presence on the field elevated the entire team, and Santos began to be recognized as one of the top clubs in South America. Pelé's influence extended beyond his goal-scoring abilities; he was a leader who inspired his teammates to perform at their best.

The young star's fame was rapidly spreading beyond Brazil. Pelé's performances in the Copa Libertadores, the most prestigious club competition in South American soccer, further enhanced his reputation. His ability to perform at the highest level against top international talent solidified his status as one of the best players in the world.

International Fame

Pelé's journey to international fame began at the 1958 World Cup in Sweden, where he emerged not just as a talented teenager but as a footballing prodigy destined to redefine the sport. At just 17, he became the youngest player in World Cup history, a record that spoke volumes about his extraordinary abilities. His performance in Sweden was the first chapter in what would become a storied World Cup legacy, marking the rise of not just a soccer star, but a global icon.

In Sweden, Pelé's talent burst onto the world stage. Initially held back in the early games, his introduction into the lineup had an immediate impact. He scored his first World Cup goal in the quarterfinals against Wales, a critical strike that sent Brazil into the semifinals. But it was in the semifinals and final where Pelé truly captivated the global audience. His hat-trick against France in the semifinals showcased his remarkable skill and poise under pressure. In the final against Sweden, Pelé's two goals, especially the famous lob over a defender followed by a volley into the net, exemplified his extraordinary ability to combine creativity, technique, and composure. With these performances, Pelé didn't just help Brazil win its first World Cup; he also etched his name into soccer history.

The 1962 World Cup in Chile offered a different narrative for Pelé. He started the tournament with a stunning goal against Mexico, displaying his characteristic brilliance. However, his journey was cut

short by an injury in the second game against Czechoslovakia. Despite this setback, Pelé's early contributions and the strength of the Brazilian squad were enough to secure a second consecutive World Cup victory. Even in his absence on the field, his presence was a beacon of inspiration for the team.

The 1966 World Cup in England was perhaps the most challenging phase of Pelé's international career. High expectations were placed on him, but the tournament turned sour as he became the target of excessively rough play by opponents. This aggressive marking led to an injury that again curtailed his participation, and Brazil was eliminated in the group stage. The disappointment of 1966, however, set the stage for a remarkable comeback.

In 1970, Pelé arrived in Mexico for his final World Cup, determined to leave an indelible mark. He led what is often regarded as the greatest team ever assembled in World Cup history. Throughout the tournament, Pelé was in sublime form, showcasing not just his scoring prowess but also his playmaking abilities. He scored a fantastic opening goal against Czechoslovakia, demonstrating his enduring skill and vision. One of his most celebrated moments came in the semifinal against Uruguay, where his audacious attempt to score without touching the ball – known as the 'Pelé runaround move' – stunned audiences worldwide. In the final against Italy, Pelé's opening goal, a perfectly executed header, set the tone for a 4-1 victory. Brazil's triumph in Mexico was a testament to Pelé's genius, earning them the right to keep the Jules Rimet Trophy permanently.

Pelé's World Cup journey was more than a series of matches; it was a narrative of a young talent rising to the pinnacle of the sport, facing setbacks, and then reaching the zenith of his career with grace and brilliance. His performances in the World Cup transcended the realm of sports, capturing the imagination of millions around the globe. Pelé's legacy in the World Cup is not just measured in goals and victories but in the way he changed soccer forever. He brought a new artistry to the game, played with an infectious joy, and demonstrated that sports could be a powerful force for bringing people together. Pelé's international fame was a beacon that illuminated the world of soccer, inspiring countless players and fans and cementing his status as one of the greatest, if not the greatest, soccer player of all time.

Legacy

Pelé's impact on soccer is immeasurable, transcending statistics and records. As he retired from professional soccer, his influence extended far beyond the pitch, cementing his status not only as a legendary athlete but also as a global ambassador for the sport and a symbol of inspiration across various domains.

Impact on Soccer

Pelé revolutionized soccer with his unparalleled skill, creativity, and intelligence. He redefined what it meant to be an attacking player, combining technical finesse, extraordinary vision, and an exceptional goal-scoring ability. His style of play influenced generations of players, encouraging a more attacking, fluid, and dynamic form of soccer. Pelé's ability to draw crowds and generate excitement about the sport significantly contributed to its global popularity. He made soccer more than just a game; he turned it into a spectacle of artistry and joy.

Moreover, Pelé's career served as a template for professional athletes in soccer and other sports. His professionalism, dedication to the game, and sportsmanship set high standards for future players. Pelé was not just a player; he was an icon that embodied the beauty and spirit of soccer.

Post-Retirement Activities

After hanging up his boots, Pelé did not step away from the spotlight but continued to contribute to the world of soccer and beyond. He took on various roles, including a stint as a minister of sports in Brazil, where he advocated for policies to promote sports and physical education. His advocacy work extended to social and humanitarian causes. Pelé worked with the United Nations and other organizations, focusing on environmental issues and children's rights, leveraging his fame to bring attention to important global issues.

Pelé also remained closely connected to soccer through ambassadorial roles. He was often seen at major soccer events, sharing his insights and spreading his love for the game. His autobiography and documentary films about his life helped to inspire and educate new generations about his journey and the broader context of soccer in the 20th century.

Global Influence

Pelé's charm, charisma, and humble background made him a relatable and admired figure worldwide. He bridged cultural and political divides, bringing people together through the universal language of soccer. Pelé's appeal went beyond soccer fans; he became a symbol of hope and possibility for millions, particularly in developing countries. His story of rising from poverty to global stardom provided a powerful narrative of determination and success against the odds.

In popular culture, Pelé's name became synonymous with excellence in soccer. Phrases like "the Pelé of..." became a common way to describe the best in any field. His influence was seen in films, music, and art, making him a cultural icon. Pelé's impact was also evident in the marketing world, where his endorsement was sought after by numerous brands, thus paving the way for future athletes to engage in lucrative sponsorships.

Legacy in Soccer and Beyond

Pelé's legacy is enduring. He is not just remembered for the goals he scored or the titles he won but for the way he played the game and the joy he brought to millions. His legacy extends to the values he represented - excellence, joy, and the power of sports to make a positive impact on society. He inspired countless individuals to pursue their dreams, whether in sports or other areas of life.

Pelé's legacy is multifaceted. As a player, he set new standards and brought a new aesthetic to soccer. Off the field, he used his fame to advocate for social causes and remained a steadfast ambassador for the sport. Globally, his influence went beyond soccer, making him a cultural and humanitarian icon. Pelé's journey from the streets of Brazil to the pinnacle of international fame is a testament to his extraordinary talent, his unwavering dedication, and his profound impact on the world.

On December 29, 2022, Pelé passed away after battling colon cancer, resulting in multiple organ failure. His tenacious spirit, both on and off the field, leaves an indelible legacy that extends far beyond soccer, inspiring countless individuals worldwide.

Mia Hamm's Dedication

Biography

Mia Hamm, a name synonymous with excellence in women's soccer, stands as an epitome of dedication and passion for the sport. Her journey from a young, enthusiastic player to becoming one of the greatest female soccer players of all time is a tale of relentless dedication, influenced significantly by her early life and family.

Born Mariel Margaret Hamm on March 17, 1972, in Selma, Alabama, Mia was the fourth of six children in a military family. Her father, Bill Hamm, a United States Air Force pilot, and her mother, Stephanie, played pivotal roles in nurturing her early interest in sports. The Hamm family moved frequently due to Bill's military assignments, which meant a constantly changing environment for the young Mia. However, this nomadic lifestyle inadvertently fostered a sense of adaptability and resilience in her, traits that would later become hallmarks of her soccer career.

From a very young age, Mia exhibited a natural affinity for sports, a trait encouraged and shared by her entire family. Her parents were supportive, but it was her older brother, Garrett, who would have a profound influence on her. Garrett, who loved soccer, introduced Mia to the game, and she quickly developed a passion for it. The backyard games they played together were not just sibling bonding moments but the foundation of Mia's soccer education. Garrett's encouragement and belief in her abilities played a crucial role in her pursuit of soccer, instilling in her the confidence and drive necessary to excel.

Mia's talent for soccer became evident early on. At the age of five, she started playing in a local soccer league. Despite being the only girl in the league initially, she quickly stood out for her skill and determination. Her competitive spirit was apparent; she did not just want to participate, she wanted to excel. This tenacity would become a defining feature of her approach to soccer and life.

As Mia grew, her family's support continued to be a cornerstone of her development. Her father's military discipline and her mother's nurturing nature provided a balanced environment where Mia's talent could thrive. They encouraged her to pursue her passion for soccer, but also emphasized the importance of education and personal development. This holistic approach to her upbringing played a crucial role in shaping her as a person and an athlete.

In high school, Mia's soccer career began to take a more defined shape. She played for Notre Dame Catholic High School in Wichita Falls, Texas, where her extraordinary abilities truly began to shine. She led her high school team to state championships, earning individual accolades along the way. Her performances in high school caught the attention of national team scouts, setting the stage for her future in soccer.

Mia's early exposure to diverse cultures and environments, thanks to her family's military background, also contributed to her development. She learned to adapt to different situations, a skill that proved invaluable in her soccer career, both on and off the field. This adaptability, combined with her natural talent and relentless work ethic, prepared her for the challenges and opportunities that lay ahead in her journey to becoming a soccer legend.

Collegiate and National Team Success

Mia Hamm's collegiate and national team careers are chapters of extraordinary achievements and pioneering successes, marking her as one of the most influential figures in women's soccer. Her time at the University of North Carolina (UNC) and with the U.S. Women's National Team (USWNT) saw her set new standards in the sport, inspiring a generation of female athletes.

University of North Carolina

Mia Hamm joined the University of North Carolina at Chapel Hill in 1989, a decision that would have a profound impact on both her career and collegiate women's soccer. At UNC, she played under the legendary coach Anson Dorrance, a figure instrumental in shaping her into an elite player. The environment at UNC, known for its rigorous training and competitive spirit, was perfect for Hamm's growth.

During her time with the Tar Heels, Hamm's impact was immediate and profound. Her extraordinary skill, combined with her work ethic and competitive drive, made her a standout player. From 1989 to 1993, she helped lead the team to four consecutive NCAA Women's Soccer Championships. Her tenure at UNC was marked by numerous individual accolades, including being named the Atlantic Coast Conference (ACC) Female Athlete of the Year for three years in a row.

Hamm's collegiate career was not just about personal achievements; she was a team player, always putting the team's success above individual glory. Her leadership on the field and ability to inspire her teammates were as crucial to the team's success as her goals and assists. She left UNC holding several records and set a high bar for future players, not just in terms of skill, but also in sportsmanship and dedication to the team.

U.S. Women's National Team

Mia Hamm's contributions to the USWNT are nothing short of legendary. She made her debut for the national team in 1987, at just 15 years old, becoming the youngest player ever to play for the team. This early start marked the beginning of a career that would significantly impact women's soccer globally.

Hamm's tenure with the USWNT was marked by unparalleled success. She played a pivotal role in the team's victories at two FIFA Women's World Cup championships (1991, 1999) and two Olympic gold medals (1996, 2004). Her performance in these tournaments showcased not only her remarkable skill and goal-scoring ability but also her vision, playmaking, and leadership qualities.

The 1999 FIFA Women's World Cup, held in the United States, was a defining moment in Hamm's career and the history of women's soccer. Her leadership and performance helped propel the USWNT to victory, capturing the hearts and imaginations of millions and bringing  unprecedented attention to women's soccer. The iconic image of the team celebrating their penalty shootout victory in the final against China features Hamm as a central figure.

Throughout her international career, Hamm set numerous records, including becoming the all-time leading scorer in international soccer - a record she held for several years. Her accolades with the USWNT are numerous, but her impact transcended numbers. She was a role model and an inspiration, showing what women could achieve in soccer and sports in general.

In both her collegiate and national team careers, Mia Hamm exemplified excellence. Her achievements with the University of North Carolina and the U.S. Women's National Team are milestones in the history of women's soccer. Hamm's legacy in these spheres is not just about the goals she scored or the titles she won, but about the path she paved for future generations of female athletes. Her dedication, skill, and passion for the game raised the profile of women's soccer and showed the world the heights women can reach in sports.

Records and Recognition

Mia Hamm's illustrious soccer career is marked by a plethora of records and recognitions, underscoring her status as one of the greatest female soccer players of all time. Her achievements on the field are paralleled by her significant role in popularizing women's soccer in the United States and around the world.

Breaking Records

Mia Hamm's name is synonymous with record-breaking feats in women's soccer. During her career, she set numerous records, many of which stood for years, showcasing her exceptional skill and longevity in the sport. One of her most notable records was becoming the all-time leading scorer in international soccer, with 158 career goals, a record she held until 2013. This achievement was not just a milestone in women's soccer but in the sport as a whole, as it surpassed the goal tallies of even the most prolific male players of her time.

In addition to her goal-scoring record, Hamm also held the record for the most international appearances or caps for the United States, with 275. This achievement highlighted her enduring presence in the national team and her consistent high-level performances over the years. Hamm's ability to maintain such a high standard over a prolonged period is a testament to her dedication, physical fitness, and mental toughness.

Accolades and Awards

Mia Hamm's list of accolades is extensive. She was twice named FIFA World Player of the Year, in 2001 and 2002, an award recognizing the best female soccer player in the world. This recognition was a fitting tribute to her impact on the sport. In the United States, she was awarded the U.S. Soccer Female Athlete of the Year five times, further cementing her status as an American soccer icon.

Her collegiate achievements at the University of North Carolina were equally impressive, including multiple All-American selections and winning the Hermann Trophy as the nation's top collegiate female soccer player. These collegiate honors were early indicators of the impact Hamm would have on the sport.

Popularizing Women's Soccer

Beyond her records and personal accolades, Mia Hamm played a pivotal role in popularizing women's soccer in the U.S. and globally. Her presence on the U.S. Women's National Team helped elevate the team's profile and brought significant attention to women's soccer. Hamm was not just a player; she was a figurehead, a symbol of the sport's growing popularity and acceptance.

The 1999 FIFA Women's World Cup, which the U.S. hosted and won, was a watershed moment in women's sports, and Hamm was at the forefront of this revolution. The tournament drew unprecedented media coverage and set attendance records, including over 90,000 spectators at the final. Hamm, with her exceptional play and marketable persona, was central to this surge in popularity. She became a household name, inspiring countless young girls to take up soccer and sparking greater interest in women's sports overall.

Hamm's impact extended beyond the field. She became involved in various endorsement deals, becoming one of the first female athletes to break into the mainstream of sports marketing. Her visibility in advertisements and media appearances played a crucial role in bringing women's soccer into the public eye. Hamm used her fame to advocate for the sport, pushing for more opportunities and better conditions for female soccer players.

Moreover, Hamm's influence was felt in the establishment of professional women's soccer leagues in the United States. Her success and popularity were instrumental in demonstrating the viability and potential of professional women's soccer, leading to the formation and growth of leagues like the Women's United Soccer Association and later the National Women's Soccer League.

Post-Retirement

Mia Hamm's retirement from professional soccer in 2004 marked the end of an extraordinary playing career, but it also signaled the beginning of a new chapter where her impact continued to resonate both within and beyond the world of sports. Her post-retirement life has been characterized by significant charity work, continued influence on young female athletes, and contributions to the growth and development of soccer.

Charity Work and Philanthropy

One of the most remarkable aspects of Hamm's post-retirement life is her dedication to philanthropic efforts. In 1999, she established the Mia Hamm Foundation in memory of her brother, Garrett, who passed away from complications of aplastic anemia. The foundation focuses on two main objectives: raising funds and awareness for bone marrow and cord blood transplants, and promoting and developing opportunities for young women in sports. Through her foundation, Hamm has made a substantial impact, hosting charity events, soccer clinics, and fundraisers, all aimed at supporting these causes.

Her commitment to helping those in need extends beyond her foundation. Hamm has been actively involved in various other charitable initiatives, including international relief efforts and programs that support families and children. Her role in these activities highlights her dedication to using her platform and influence to make a positive difference in the world.

Influence on Young Female Athletes

Mia's influence on young female athletes has been profound and enduring. As a pioneer in women's soccer, she has inspired countless girls to pursue their dreams in sports. Hamm has been actively involved in promoting and supporting women's soccer at all levels.

15

She often participates in soccer clinics, camps, and speaking engagements, where she shares her experiences and insights, inspiring the next generation of female athletes.

Hamm's impact on young athletes extends beyond her physical presence. Her story of dedication, resilience, and success resonates with many young girls who see her as a role model. Her legacy has encouraged more girls to participate in sports, contributing to the growth of women's soccer and other sports at the grassroots level.

Contributions to Soccer and Sports Commentating

Following her retirement, Hamm has continued to contribute to the growth and development of soccer. She has been involved in various capacities, including serving on the board of directors for AS Roma, a professional Italian soccer club. Her insights and experiences have been valuable in promoting the sport and advocating for the development of women's soccer globally.

Hamm has also ventured into sports commentating, providing analysis and commentary for soccer matches. Her knowledge of the game and articulate expression have made her a respected figure in sports broadcasting, further extending her influence in the world of soccer.

Authorship and Public Speaking

Hamm has authored books, including "Go For the Goal: A Champion's Guide To Winning In Soccer And Life," where she shares her journey and insights into soccer. These works serve as an inspiration and guide for young athletes and soccer enthusiasts. Additionally, her role as a public speaker has seen her share her experiences and perspectives, motivating and encouraging diverse audiences.

Legacy and Continuing Impact

Mia Hamm's post-retirement activities have solidified her status not just as a legendary soccer player, but as a philanthropist, role model, and advocate for women in sports. Her ongoing involvement in charity, mentorship of young athletes, and contributions to soccer demonstrate her unwavering dedication to the sport and her commitment to making a positive impact in the lives of others.

Hamm's life after retirement reflects the same passion and drive that she exhibited on the soccer field. She continues to inspire, lead, and contribute significantly to various spheres, ensuring that her legacy extends far beyond her achievements as a soccer player. Mia Hamm remains an influential figure, whose life and work continue to motivate and shape the world of sports and beyond.

Mohamed Salah: From Nagrig to Stardom

Early Life

Mohamed Salah's journey from the small village of Nagrig in Egypt to the pinnacle of global football stardom is a story of dedication, talent, and the relentless pursuit of a dream. His early life in Nagrig lays the foundation of this remarkable journey, reflecting the humble beginnings from which one of the world's most celebrated footballers emerged.

Growing Up in Nagrig, Egypt

Mohamed Salah Hamed Mahrous Ghaly was born on June 15, 1992, in the village of Nagrig, located in the Gharbia Governorate in Egypt. His family, while not affluent, was deeply supportive of his passion for football. Nagrig, a rural village far from the bustling cityscapes of Cairo or Alexandria, provided a modest and close-knit community backdrop for Salah's early years.

From a young age, Salah displayed an innate love for football. His early life revolved around the game, playing with friends in the streets and open spaces of his village. The local football pitch became a second home to him, where he spent countless hours honing his skills. Salah's early play was characterized by the raw talent and determination that would later define his professional career.

Early Influences and Inspirations

Salah's passion for football was fueled by the football culture in Egypt, where the sport is a beloved national pastime. He grew up idolizing Egyptian and African football stars, drawing inspiration from their success and dreaming of one day emulating their achievements. Salah's family, particularly his father, played a crucial role in nurturing his talent. Despite the challenges of providing for a family in a modest village, Salah's parents went to great lengths to support his football aspirations, recognizing their son's exceptional talent.

Journey to Organized Football

Salah's journey to organized football began at a young age. He joined the youth team of his local club, El Mokawloon, also known as Arab Contractors, based in Cairo. This step marked the beginning of his formal journey in football, but it also presented significant challenges. The young Salah had to endure long and exhausting commutes from Nagrig to Cairo for training and matches, often traveling several hours each way. The commitment and sacrifices made during these early years were testaments to his dedication and the support of his family.

Despite the physical and mental toll of these demanding commutes, Salah's performance at El Mokawloon did not go unnoticed. He quickly progressed through the ranks, showcasing his exceptional speed, agility, and goal-scoring ability. His talent shone in the youth leagues, and it wasn't long before he was called up to join the senior team, setting him on the path to professional football.

Early Challenges

The challenges and experiences of Salah's early life in Nagrig played a significant role in shaping his character and approach to football. The humility, work ethic, and resilience that are hallmarks of his personality can be traced back to his upbringing in a modest village environment. His journey from Nagrig to the professional football stage is not just a story of sporting success; it's a narrative of overcoming odds, staying grounded despite fame, and maintaining a strong connection to one's roots.

Career Progression

Early Professional Career in Egypt

Salah's professional football journey began with El Mokawloon (Arab Contractors) in the Egyptian Premier League. Joining their senior team in 2010, he quickly made an impression with his speed, dribbling skills, and goal-scoring ability. His standout performances in the Egyptian league and his potential as a future star were evident. However, his time in Egypt's top league was cut short by the suspension of the league following the Port Said Stadium riot in 2012. This unfortunate event inadvertently set the stage for Salah's move to Europe.

Move to FC Basel in Switzerland

Salah's talents caught the attention of European scouts, and in April 2012, he signed with Swiss club FC Basel. This move was Salah's first foray into European football, representing a significant step in his career. At Basel, he developed further, honing his skills and adapting to the European style of play. Salah helped the team win the Swiss Super League in his first season, and his performances in the UEFA Champions League and UEFA Europa League showcased his abilities on a larger stage. His pace, skill, and flair were instrumental in Basel's domestic success and their competitive performances in European competitions.

Transition to the Italian Serie A

Salah's next move was to one of Europe's top leagues, the Italian Serie A. Initially, he joined Chelsea in the English Premier League in 2014 but struggled to secure a regular place in the first team. Subsequently, he was loaned to Fiorentina, Italy, in February 2015. In Italy, Salah found a league that suited his playing style. He thrived at Fiorentina, rediscovering his confidence and form. His impact was immediate and significant, with impressive performances that rejuvenated his career.

After a successful stint at Fiorentina, Salah moved to another Serie A club, AS Roma, initially on loan and then permanently. At Roma, he elevated his game further, becoming one of the league's standout players. He was a key figure in Roma's attack, contributing significantly in terms of goals and assists. His two seasons at Roma solidified his reputation as one of the top wingers in European football.

Stardom at Liverpool in the English Premier League

Salah's impressive performances in Italy led to a transfer to Liverpool FC in the English Premier League in 2017. This move marked a turning point in his career. Under the management of Jürgen Klopp, Salah evolved into one of the world's best players. In his first season at Liverpool, he broke the Premier League record for the most goals in a 38-game season, scoring 32 goals. His speed, movement, and clinical finishing made him a key component of Liverpool's potent attack and helped the club reach the UEFA Champions League final in his first season.

Salah's impact at Liverpool has been profound. He has consistently been one of the Premier League's top scorers and has played a crucial role in Liverpool's successes, including winning the UEFA Champions League in 2019 and the Premier League in 2020. His performances have earned him numerous individual awards and accolades, cementing his status as one of the elite players in the game.

Legacy and Influence

Mohamed Salah's career progression from Egypt to the pinnacle of European football is a testament to his exceptional talent, work ethic, and determination. His journey is inspirational, highlighting the possibilities that arise from perseverance and adaptability. Salah has not only achieved individual success but has also become a symbol of hope and pride for millions, particularly in the Middle East and Africa.

On-field Achievements

Mohamed Salah's career, adorned with numerous on-field achievements and accolades, narrates a story of a footballer who not only reached the apex of the sport but also redefined the role of a winger with his unique blend of speed, skill, and scoring ability. His journey through various top leagues in Europe has been marked by key moments and awards that underscore his status as one of the contemporary greats of the game.

Explosive Impact at FC Basel

Salah's European journey started with a bang at FC Basel, where his performance against Chelsea in the UEFA Europa League put him on the map as a rising star in European football. His contributions were pivotal in Basel's Swiss Super League victories in 2012-2013 and 2013-2014, showcasing his ability to perform on both domestic and European stages.

Rising Star in Italy

Salah's stint in the Italian Serie A, first with Fiorentina and then with AS Roma, saw him evolve into a top-tier football talent. At Fiorentina, he scored nine goals in 26 appearances, an impressive feat that earned him the admiration of the Fiorentina fans and wider recognition in Italian football. His time at AS Roma was even more fruitful; he was the team's top scorer in the 2016-2017 season, with 15 goals in Serie A and a total of 19 in all competitions. His performances at Roma solidified his reputation as a lethal winger, combining his blistering pace with a newfound composure in front of goal.

Record-Breaking Tenure at Liverpool

Salah's transfer to Liverpool in 2017 marked the beginning of what would be a record-breaking tenure. In his debut season (2017-2018), he scored 44 goals in all competitions, breaking numerous records. Most notably, he set a new Premier League record for the most goals (32) in a 38-game season. This extraordinary feat earned him the Premier League Golden Boot and the PFA Players' Player of the Year award.

His first season at Liverpool also saw him lead the team to the UEFA Champions League final, an achievement that underscored his importance to the team. Though Liverpool did not win the final, Salah's contributions throughout the tournament were critical.

The following seasons saw Salah maintain his high standards. He won the Premier League Golden Boot again in the 2018-2019 season, this time sharing it with Sadio Mané and Pierre-Emerick Aubameyang. He played a key role in Liverpool's 2018-2019 UEFA Champions League triumph, scoring in the final against Tottenham Hotspur. This victory was a sweet redemption for Salah and Liverpool, marking the club's sixth European Cup/Champions League title.

In the 2019-2020 season, Salah helped Liverpool win their first Premier League title in 30 years. His consistent performances and crucial goals throughout the season were instrumental in ending Liverpool's long wait for the coveted league title.

International Success with Egypt

Salah's achievements extend to his international career with the Egyptian national team. He was instrumental in Egypt's qualification for the 2018 FIFA World Cup, their first since 1990. His penalty kick against Congo in a crucial qualifier secured Egypt's place in the tournament. Although injury hampered his World Cup performance, his presence was a source of national pride.

Individual Awards and Recognitions

Salah's individual accolades are a testament to his extraordinary talent. He has been named the African Footballer of the Year multiple times, reflecting his status as one of the continent's finest exports. His inclusion in the FIFA FIFPro World11, UEFA Team of the Year, and being awarded the BBC African Footballer of the Year multiple times further affirm his standing in global football.

Influence on the Game

Mohamed Salah's on-field achievements have not only earned him individual accolades but have also left a significant impact on the game. He has redefined what is expected of a winger, combining traditional wing play with prolific goal-scoring. His style has influenced how attackers are utilized in modern football tactics, blending speed, skill, and scoring ability in a way that few others have managed.

Off-field Influence

Philanthropy and Community Involvement

Salah's philanthropic endeavors are deeply rooted in his upbringing and connection to his hometown, Nagrig. He has consistently given back to his community, investing in essential infrastructure and services. Notably, Salah has funded the construction of a medical center and school in Nagrig, significantly improving access to healthcare and education for the local population. His contributions also include donations to the National Cancer Institute in Cairo following a terrorist attack in 2019, as well as support for various charitable organizations and initiatives in Egypt.

His philanthropic efforts extend beyond tangible contributions. Salah has used his platform to raise awareness for various causes, including mental health and children's rights. He has been actively involved in campaigns and initiatives that seek to improve the lives of underprivileged children in Egypt and across the world.

Influence on Perceptions of Muslim Athletes

Salah's impact as one of the most prominent Muslim athletes globally is profound. His success at the highest level of football and his public expression of faith have contributed to changing perceptions of Muslim athletes in sport. His goal celebrations often include sujood, the Islamic act of prostration, which he has performed on some of the biggest stages in football. This visibility has been instrumental in normalizing the expression of faith in the sports arena, fostering a greater understanding and acceptance of cultural and religious diversity.

His influence in this regard has been the subject of academic study, with researchers from the University of Stanford finding that Salah's presence in Liverpool has been linked to a significant reduction in Islamophobic behaviors and hate crimes in the area. His impact goes beyond tolerance, actively fostering a sense of inclusivity and respect for cultural and religious diversity.

Role as a National Icon in Egypt

In Egypt, Salah is more than just a football player; he is a national icon and a source of immense pride. His rise from a small village to global stardom resonates deeply with the Egyptian people, representing a story of hope, determination, and success against the odds. Salah is not only celebrated for his achievements on the pitch but also revered for his humility, work ethic, and dedication to his country.

Salah's influence in Egypt transcends sports. He is seen as a role model and an ambassador for the country, embodying the potential of Egyptian talent and the spirit of perseverance. His performances with the Egyptian national team, particularly during the 2018 World Cup qualifiers, united the country in a shared sense of national pride and joy.

His role as a national icon is also evident in his involvement in various national campaigns and initiatives. Salah has been at the forefront of campaigns promoting health, education, and social welfare in Egypt. His voice and image carry significant weight, and he has used this influence to advocate for positive change and development in his home country.

Global Ambassador

Mohamed Salah's off-field influence has established him as a global ambassador for various causes. Through his philanthropy, he has impacted the lives of many, particularly in Egypt. His status as a prominent Muslim athlete has contributed to breaking down stereotypes and fostering a more inclusive and respectful sporting environment. As a national icon, he continues to inspire and uplift millions, proving that sports figures can be powerful agents of social change and cultural understanding.

Japan's 2011 World Cup Comeback

Before the World Cup

The story of Japan's women's national football team, affectionately known as "Nadeshiko Japan," and their triumphant journey in the 2011 FIFA Women's World Cup is not just a sports narrative but a tale of resilience and hope. The backdrop to their World Cup campaign was marked by unprecedented challenges, both on and off the field, particularly the devastating impact of the earthquake and tsunami that struck Japan in March 2011.

The Devastating Earthquake and Tsunami of March 2011

In March 2011, just months before the World Cup in Germany, Japan was hit by one of the most catastrophic natural disasters in its history. A massive 9.0 magnitude earthquake, followed by a devastating tsunami, struck the Tohoku region in northeastern Japan. The disaster resulted in significant loss of life and widespread destruction, deeply affecting the entire nation.

For the Japanese women's football team, this tragedy had profound implications. Several players had personal connections to the affected areas, and the disaster struck close to home, bringing a sense of grief and sorrow. The calamity disrupted their preparation for the World Cup, as the nation grappled with the aftermath and the team members dealt with the emotional impact of the disaster.

Challenges in Preparation and Training

Prior to the 2011 World Cup, the Nadeshiko Japan team faced numerous challenges in their preparation. The women's football program in Japan, despite having made strides in the preceding years, still lacked the extensive support and resources found in some of their international counterparts' programs. The team's preparation was further hampered by the disaster, which necessitated a shift in focus and resources towards national recovery efforts.

Training camps and scheduled international matches were disrupted, complicating their tactical and physical preparations. The players, while deeply affected by the national tragedy, had to find a way to focus on their football amidst the prevailing sense of loss and rebuilding.

Underdog Status and Prior World Cup Performances

Heading into the 2011 World Cup, Japan was not considered among the favorites to win the tournament. Historically, the team had respectable showings in previous World Cups but had never progressed beyond the quarterfinals. The world's football community viewed Japan as a competent side but not as a serious contender for the title.

This underdog status was compounded by the emotional weight the team carried into the tournament. They were not just playing for footballing glory but also as representatives of a nation in mourning, carrying the hopes and emotions of millions of Japanese people seeking a semblance of joy and normalcy after the disaster.

The Spirit of Resilience and Determination

In the face of these challenges, the spirit of the Japanese team was remarkable. They rallied around the adversity, channeling their grief into determination and resilience. The players and coaching staff, led by Norio Sasaki, adopted a mindset of playing for their nation, viewing their participation in the World Cup as a means to uplift the spirits of their countrymen and women.

As they departed for Germany, the Nadeshiko Japan team was not merely a group of footballers; they were a symbol of national resilience and hope. The adversity they faced before the World Cup forged a strong sense of unity and purpose, setting the stage for what would become one of the most inspirational stories in the history of sports.

Group Stage and Knockout Rounds

Group Stage Performances

Japan was placed in Group B alongside New Zealand, Mexico, and England. The group stage was crucial in setting the tone for their campaign, and Japan approached it with a mix of strategic acumen and technical proficiency.

Japan's World Cup campaign began against New Zealand. In a tightly contested match, Japan emerged victorious with a narrow 2-1 win. Aya Miyama and Yūki Nagasato scored for Japan, showcasing the team's attacking flair and tactical discipline. This victory was crucial in building confidence and momentum for the team.

Their next match was against Mexico, a team known for its physical style of play. Japan demonstrated their technical superiority and tactical intelligence, securing a comfortable 4-0 win. This match was evidence of Japan's attacking prowess, with Homare Sawa, the team captain, scoring a hat-trick.

The final group match against England was a tougher challenge. Despite a 2-0 defeat, Japan had shown enough quality and resilience in their previous games to progress to the knockout stage as one of the best third-placed teams. This match was a learning experience, preparing them for the challenges ahead.

Knockout Round Heroics

The knockout stages were where Japan truly showcased their championship mettle, facing and overcoming some of the strongest teams in women's football.

Japan faced a formidable challenge against the host nation, Germany, in the quarterfinals. The German team, two-time defending champions, were favorites, but Japan executed a perfect tactical game. In a display of disciplined defending and patient play, Japan managed to take the  game to extra time. In a dramatic turn of events, Karina Maruyama scored in the 108th minute, securing a historic 1-0 win for Japan. This victory was more than just a soccer triumph; it was a statement to the world about the spirit and quality of Japanese women's football.

Riding high on confidence, Japan faced Sweden in the semifinals. Sweden took an early lead, but Japan's resilience shone through once again. They responded with three unanswered goals, with Nahomi Kawasumi scoring twice and Homare Sawa adding another. The 3-1 comeback victory showcased their tactical flexibility and mental strength.

The Final Against the USA

The final of the 2011 FIFA Women's World Cup between Japan and the United States was not just a clash of two footballing powerhouses; it was a showcase of resilience, teamwork, and the indomitable spirit of Nadeshiko Japan. Played on July 17, 2011, in Frankfurt, Germany, this final was a dramatic, emotionally charged encounter that etched itself into the annals of football history.

Setting the Stage

The United States, a dominant force in women's football, entered the final as favorites. They boasted a team full of talent and experience and were determined to reclaim the World Cup trophy. Japan, on the other hand, was riding a wave of unexpected success, having defeated two of the tournament's favorites, Germany and Sweden, in the knockout stages. For Japan, this final was more than a match; it was a symbol of hope and resilience for a nation still reeling from the devastating earthquake and tsunami.

Early American Dominance

The match started with the United States asserting their dominance. The American team's physicality, speed, and tactical acumen posed a significant challenge for Japan. The U.S. created numerous scoring opportunities but were initially denied by the heroics of Japanese goalkeeper Ayumi Kaihori and Japan's disciplined defense. Japan's strategy was focused on maintaining their shape, absorbing pressure, and looking for opportunities to counter-attack.

Japan's Resilience on Display

The deadlock was finally broken in the 69th minute when the U.S. scored through Alex Morgan. However, in what would become the theme of the night, Japan's resilience shone through. Aya Miyama capitalized on a defensive lapse to score an equalizer in the 81st minute, bringing Japan level and sending a wave of belief through the team.

Extra Time and Further Drama

The match went into extra time, and once again, the United States took the lead with a goal from Abby Wambach in the 104th minute. It seemed like the U.S. had secured the victory, but Japan had other ideas. With just three minutes left in extra time, Homare Sawa, the inspirational captain of Nadeshiko Japan, scored a remarkable equalizer, redirecting a corner kick into the net. Sawa's goal, her fifth of the tournament, not only brought Japan level but also epitomized the team's never-say-die attitude.

The Penalty Shootout

The final was destined to be decided by a penalty shootout. Japan's composure and teamwork were once again on display. While the U.S. faltered under pressure, missing their first three penalties, Japan was clinical. After successful conversions by Miyama, Nagasato, and Sakaguchi, it was Saki Kumagai who stepped up to take the decisive penalty. She calmly slotted the ball past the American goalkeeper, securing a historic victory for Japan.

The final whistle marked the culmination of a remarkable journey for Nadeshiko Japan. Their victory in the 2011 Women's World Cup was a story of tactical brilliance, incredible resilience, and unyielding teamwork. The Japanese team's ability to overcome adversity, not just in the final but throughout the tournament, resonated deeply, both at home and across the globe.

Impact and Legacy

A Beacon of Hope in the Wake of Tragedy

In March 2011, Japan was struck by one of the most catastrophic natural disasters in its history. The earthquake and tsunami resulted in immense loss and suffering, casting a shadow of grief and despair across the nation. In this context, the success of Nadeshiko Japan in the World Cup took on a greater significance. It provided a much-needed source of joy and pride for a country in mourning and in the process of rebuilding.

The team's resilience and fighting spirit on the global stage mirrored the resilience of the Japanese people facing the aftermath of the disaster. Their victory was seen as emblematic of the nation's ability to rise from adversity and rebuild. It offered a narrative of hope and positive change, crucial for the nation's morale during a time of national crisis.

Cultural and Social Impact in Japan

In Japan, the victory had a profound cultural and social impact. It challenged traditional gender norms and perceptions regarding women in sports and society. The success of Nadeshiko Japan brought increased attention and respect to women's sports, which historically had received less recognition and support compared to men's sports in the country.

The triumph spurred a surge in the popularity of women's football and sports participation among girls and young women. It inspired a generation of female athletes, showing them the possibilities and heights that could be achieved. The team's success also led to increased investment and development in women's sports infrastructure and programs across the nation.

Global Resonance and Changing Perceptions

Globally, Japan's victory in the World Cup had a significant impact on how women's football was perceived. It demonstrated that success in the sport was not confined to the traditional powerhouses of North America and Europe. Japan's tactical finesse, technical skill, and team-oriented play offered a different and successful approach to the game, broadening the tactical and stylistic diversity in women's football.

The team's story and their journey to World Cup glory captured the hearts of football fans and non-fans alike around the world. It was a story that transcended cultural and linguistic barriers, highlighting the unifying power of sport. The victory served as an inspiration, showing that with determination, teamwork, and resilience, underdogs could achieve the highest levels of success.

Legacy of Nadeshiko Japan's Triumph

The legacy of Japan's victory in the 2011 World Cup continues to be felt in various ways. It remains a shining example of how sports can provide solace and bring a sense of normalcy in times of crisis. The team's triumph has become a part of Japan's national story, a story of overcoming adversity that is revisited and celebrated.

In the realm of sports, the victory helped elevate the profile of women's football globally. It contributed to the growing interest and investment in women's sports worldwide, paving the way for future generations of female athletes.

The Magic of Ronaldinho

Early Life and Career Beginnings

The story of Ronaldinho, one of football's most enigmatic and talented figures, is as captivating as his play on the field. Born Ronaldo de Assis Moreira on March 21, 1980, in Porto Alegre, Brazil, Ronaldinho's journey from a young boy with a boundless passion for soccer to a global superstar encapsulates the essence of Brazilian football – skill, creativity, and an irrepressible joy for the game.

A Football-Focused Upbringing in Porto Alegre

Ronaldinho was born into a family deeply passionate about football. His father, João de Assis Moreira, was a shipyard worker and a local club footballer. Tragically, Ronaldinho's father passed away when he was just eight, but the seeds of football passion were already sown. His older brother, Roberto, was a professional footballer, offering

Ronaldinho an immediate role model and insight into the footballing world.

Growing up in the Vila Nova neighborhood of Porto Alegre, Ronaldinho's childhood was marked by financial challenges, but the joy of playing football was a constant. The streets and makeshift pitches of Porto Alegre were his first footballing schools, where his natural flair and talent began to shine. From a very young age, Ronaldinho exhibited a remarkable ability to control the ball and perform tricks that left onlookers in awe.

Youth Career and Early Recognition

Ronaldinho's talent did not go unnoticed for long. By the age of 13, he had already begun to make headlines, once scoring a staggering 23 goals in a single game, a feat that started to draw national attention. His youth career took a significant turn when he joined the ranks of Grêmio, one of Porto Alegre's biggest clubs. Here, Ronaldinho honed his skills, developing a playing style that blended technical skill with creative flair – characteristics that would become his trademarks.

At Grêmio, Ronaldinho's talent flourished. He progressed through the youth ranks quickly, demonstrating a level of skill and imagination on the pitch that was rare for players of his age. His dribbling ability, ball control, and vision were exceptional, marking him as a special talent destined for greater heights.

Professional Debut and Rise to Stardom

Ronaldinho's professional debut for Grêmio came in 1998, a moment that marked the beginning of an illustrious career. He quickly became a key player for the club, dazzling fans with his extraordinary tricks, flicks, and overall mastery of the ball. His impact was immediate and profound, helping Grêmio to win the inaugural Copa Sul-Minas.

Ronaldinho's performances at Grêmio put him on the radar of top European clubs. However, it was his performances with Brazil's national team at the youth level, particularly during the 1999 FIFA U-20 World Cup and the 1999 Copa América, that catapulted him to international recognition. His skillful play, characterized by a combination of playfulness and effectiveness, captured the imagination of football fans worldwide.

Legacy of Ronaldinho's Early Career

Ronaldinho's early career laid the foundation for what would become a legendary journey in football. From the streets of Porto Alegre to the stadiums of the world, his initial years were a testament to the magic he brought to the game. Ronaldinho not only played football; he celebrated it with every dribble, every pass, and every goal. His early life and beginnings in Brazil were reflective of a player who would go on to redefine what it meant to play with creativity, passion, and joy – the essence of the beautiful game.

Rise to Fame at PSG and Barcelona

Paris Saint-Germain: The European Debut

In 2001, Ronaldinho made the significant leap to European football by signing with Paris Saint-Germain, a move that marked the beginning of his international career. This transition was a pivotal moment for Ronaldinho, introducing him to a more competitive and demanding European football landscape. At PSG, he encountered the challenges of adapting to a new culture, language, and style of play.

Despite these challenges, Ronaldinho's talent shone through. His first season at PSG was marked by moments of brilliance, showcasing his unique blend of technical skill and creative flair. He became known for his dribbling ability, audacious tricks, and the joy with which he played the game. His impact at PSG was significant; he quickly became a fan favorite and a crucial player for the team.

Ronaldinho's time at PSG, however, was not without its difficulties. He faced disciplinary issues and clashes with the management, which somewhat overshadowed his on-field performances. Despite these setbacks, his time in Paris was instrumental in his growth as a player, preparing him for the larger stage that awaited him.

Barcelona: The Rise to Global Stardom

In 2003, Ronaldinho made a career-defining move to FC Barcelona, a club undergoing a period of rebuilding. His arrival at Barcelona was more than just a transfer; it was the beginning of an era. Under the guidance of coach Frank Rijkaard, Ronaldinho became the centerpiece of a project aimed at bringing Barcelona back to the forefront of European football.

At Barcelona, Ronaldinho's career soared to new heights. He was not just a player; he was an artist, and Camp Nou was his canvas. His first season with the club was marked by mesmerizing performances that reignited the passion of Barcelona fans. Ronaldinho's play was characterized by a sense of freedom and creativity that was infectious. He was instrumental in Barcelona's La Liga triumph in the 2004-2005 season, ending a six-year league title drought for the club.

His second season at Barcelona was even more spectacular. Ronaldinho was at the peak of his powers, and his performances on the field were a blend of artistry and effectiveness. He played a primary role in Barcelona's domestic and European success, leading the team to another La Liga title and the coveted UEFA Champions League trophy in the 2005-2006 season. His impact was recognized globally, earning him the FIFA World Player of the Year award in both 2004 and 2005.

Ronaldinho's influence extended beyond his statistical contributions. He revitalized Barcelona with his imaginative play, bringing a sense of excitement and unpredictability to the game. He was a player who could change the course of a match with a single moment of brilliance, and his smile and enthusiasm on the pitch embodied the pure joy of football.

Legacy at Barcelona

Ronaldinho's legacy at Barcelona is indelible. He was instrumental in ushering in a new era of success for the club and inspired a generation of players who followed. His style of play had a lasting impact on Barcelona's footballing philosophy, emphasizing skill, creativity, and flair. Ronaldinho's time at Barcelona is remembered not only for the trophies and accolades but for the magical moments he created and the joy he brought to fans around the world.

Playing Style and Impact

Unparalleled Creativity and Flair

Ronaldinho's approach to football was grounded in an exceptional level of creativity. He viewed the pitch as a stage and himself as an entertainer, with the ball at his feet being his tool to captivate the audience. His style was a throwback to the street soccer of his childhood in Brazil - a free, expressive, and joyful way of playing that prioritized ingenuity over functionality.

He was renowned for his repertoire of tricks, the most iconic being his elastico, a quick flick of the ball that often left defenders bewildered. Ronaldinho's ability to perform such tricks in high-stakes situations against top-tier opponents set him apart. His dribbling was not just effective but mesmerizing, often resulting in a tangible sense of anticipation and excitement among spectators whenever he received the ball.

Master of the Unexpected

One of Ronaldinho's most notable traits was his unpredictability. Defenders found him nearly impossible to read, as he could change his play style spontaneously. He could turn a seemingly benign situation into a goal-scoring opportunity with a sudden burst of speed, a clever pass, or a surprising shot. His no-look passes and behind-the-leg crosses became trademarks, reflecting his penchant for the unexpected.

Joy and Entertainment

Ronaldinho played with a smile on his face, embodying the joy and beauty of football. This sense of enjoyment was infectious and resonated deeply with fans around the globe, regardless of their team allegiances. He reminded fans that football, at its core, is a game meant to be enjoyed. His playful attitude on the pitch, combined with his extraordinary skill, made watching him an entertaining and exhilarating experience.

Impact on Teammates and Opponents

Ronaldinho's style had a significant impact on his teammates. He elevated the play of those around him, not just through his technical contributions but through his positive attitude and charisma. He was a leader in the sense that he inspired confidence and creativity among his peers, encouraging them to express themselves freely on the pitch.

His impact on opponents was equally notable. Ronaldinho earned the respect and admiration of his adversaries, many of whom have spoken about the privilege of sharing the pitch with him. His style of play, marked by respect and sportsmanship, endeared him to fellow players, further cementing his legacy in the sport.

Legacy in Football

Ronaldinho's legacy in football is defined by his unique style of play and the joy he brought to the game. He left an indelible mark on the sport, influencing a generation of players who saw in him the epitome of footballing freedom and expression. Ronaldinho redefined what it meant to be a successful footballer - it was not just about winning and statistics, but about how the game was played and experienced.

Legacy and Influence

Reviving the Artistry in Football

Ronaldinho's legacy is inextricably linked to the artistry and creativity he brought to the field. At a time when football was increasingly becoming tactical and physically demanding, Ronaldinho reminded everyone that at its heart, football was about expression, creativity, and flair. He was a throwback to the Brazilian legends of the past, embodying the 'samba style' of play that was synonymous with skillful, attacking football. Ronaldinho's impact went beyond his own achievements; he revived the romanticism of football, inspiring players and fans alike with his imaginative style of play.

Influence on Future Generations

Ronaldinho's influence on future generations of footballers cannot be overstated. He became a role model for countless young players, many of whom grew up imitating his tricks and emulating his style on playgrounds and training grounds around the world. Players like Neymar Jr., Lionel Messi, and many others have cited Ronaldinho as a major influence in their careers. His legacy is evident in the way these players approach the game, prioritizing creativity and expression in their style of play.

Beyond individual players, Ronaldinho's influence is seen in the broader footballing philosophy. He played a significant role in shaping the way football is approached and played, championing a style that values skill and inventiveness over mere physical prowess or tactical rigidity.

Importance of Playing with Passion

One of the most enduring aspects of Ronaldinho's legacy is the importance he placed on playing with passion and joy. He approached every game with a smile, showcasing a genuine love and enthusiasm for the sport. This attitude was not only refreshing but also inspirational. Ronaldinho showed that success on the football field was not just about winning; it was about enjoying the game and playing with passion. He made fans and players alike remember why they fell in love with the game in the first place.

Cultural Impact and Global Ambassadorship

Ronaldinho transcended the sport, becoming a cultural icon and a global ambassador for football. His appeal extended beyond traditional footballing nations, bringing the sport to new audiences and demographics. He was not just a footballer but a symbol of the joy and unifying power of the game. Ronaldinho's appeal bridged cultural and linguistic divides, making him one of the most recognizable and beloved figures in the sport's history.

Legacy in Football and Beyond

Ronaldinho's legacy in football is about the magical moments he created, the joy he brought to millions, and the inspiration he provided to players and fans. He will be remembered not just for his achievements and skills but for the way he played the game - with a child-like joy and an artist's flair. His career serves as a reminder that football, at its best, is an art form, and that playing with passion is as important as winning.

Since retiring from professional soccer, Ronaldinho has remained active, taking on ambassadorial roles for football organizations, engaging in charity work, and occasionally participating in exhibition matches.

The Story of the Invincibles

Team Composition and Philosophy

The 2003-2004 season of the English Premier League witnessed one of the most remarkable achievements in football history, as Arsenal FC completed an entire season unbeaten, earning them the moniker "The Invincibles." This feat was evidence of a unique blend of individual talent, innovative coaching, and a footballing philosophy that revolutionized the English game.

Arsène Wenger's Vision and Philosophy

The architect of this extraordinary achievement was French manager Arsène Wenger. Wenger, who joined Arsenal in 1996, brought a revolutionary approach to the Premier League. His philosophy emphasized skillful, attacking football, and a belief in playing the game with artistry and flair. Wenger's approach was not just about winning; it was about dominating opponents with style and grace.

Wenger was a proponent of meticulous player development, dietary regimes, and a focus on mental preparation. His methods, considered radical at the time, included detailed statistical analyses to improve performance and training techniques. Wenger's philosophy extended beyond tactics; he fostered a culture of unity, respect, and professionalism within the team.

The Invincibles' Team Composition

The composition of the team was a masterful blend of experience, youth, technical skill, and physical prowess. Each player brought a unique set of skills, contributing to a well-balanced and cohesive unit.

The defensive line, led by Sol Campbell and Kolo Touré, was formidable. Both central defenders combined physical strength with intelligent defending. Lauren and Ashley Cole, as full-backs, provided defensive solidity and an attacking threat down the wings.

The midfield was the engine room of the team. Patrick Vieira, the captain, was the heart of the squad, providing leadership, physical presence, and technical ability. Alongside him were players like Gilberto Silva, who offered defensive steel, and Freddie Ljungberg, known for his timely runs and goal-scoring ability. Robert Pires provided creativity and flair, contributing significantly to the team's attacking prowess.

In attack, Thierry Henry was the standout performer. Henry's blend of speed, skill, and finishing ability made him one of the world's best forwards. Dennis Bergkamp, the experienced Dutchman, played a crucial role, combining vision and technique to orchestrate the team's attacking play.

Jens Lehmann, the German goalkeeper, brought experience and confidence to the team, playing a key role in several crucial saves throughout the season.

Tactical Flexibility and Adaptability

One of Wenger's strengths was his tactical flexibility and ability to adapt to different opponents. The team could switch from a traditional 4-4-2 to a more fluid formation, allowing them to control the midfield and create numerous scoring opportunities. Wenger encouraged his players to express themselves on the field, resulting in a style of play that was both effective and entertaining.

Team Chemistry and Unity

The chemistry within the team was palpable. The blend of different nationalities, personalities, and playing styles created a unique dynamic. Wenger's management skills were crucial in forging a strong team spirit, with a collective belief in their ability to achieve greatness.

The Unbeaten Run

The Season's Opening

Arsenal began their season with an assertive 2-1 victory against Everton. This win set the tone for their campaign, showcasing their attacking prowess and defensive resilience. As the season progressed, Arsenal's blend of fluid attacking football and solid defending became increasingly apparent. The team displayed an exceptional blend of skill and strength, with players like Thierry Henry, Robert Pires, and Patrick Vieira in peak form.

Key Matches and Turning Points

One of the early pivotal matches was the North London derby against Tottenham Hotspur. A thrilling encounter that ended in a 2-1 victory for Arsenal, it underscored the team's resolve and ability to perform in high-pressure situations.

Another significant match was the 5-1 demolition of Inter Milan at San Siro in the Champions League. Although the Champions League was not part of the unbeaten league run, this performance against one of Europe's best teams highlighted Arsenal's quality on a global stage.

As the season unfolded, Arsenal's confidence and dominance grew. Matches against formidable opponents like Liverpool, Manchester United, and Chelsea were approached with a tactical nous and composure that emphasized their title credentials. The 2-0 victory against Liverpool at Anfield, marked by Henry's exceptional solo goal, was a standout performance and a statement of intent.

Maintaining Consistency

A key aspect of Arsenal's unbeaten run was their ability to maintain consistency, even in challenging circumstances. The team displayed remarkable mental strength, often securing victories from drawn positions or holding onto leads under pressure. Wenger's ability to rotate the squad effectively, ensuring that key players were rested and fresh, was decisive in maintaining their performance levels throughout the season.

Overcoming Challenges

The path to an unbeaten season was not without its challenges. Arsenal had to navigate through injuries, suspensions, and dips in form. The resilience to bounce back from setbacks was evident in matches like the draw against Manchester United at Old Trafford. Arsenal faced intense pressure but managed to secure a 0-0 draw, with a memorable penalty save by Jens Lehmann from Ruud van Nistelrooy.

The Final Stretch

As the season neared its end, the pressure of maintaining the unbeaten record grew. However, Arsenal showed composure and maturity in handling the expectations. A crucial victory came against Tottenham in late April, where a 2-2 draw at White Hart Lane was enough to secure the Premier League title, confirming their status as champions with four games to spare.

Arsenal concluded the season unbeaten, with 26 wins and 12 draws, a feat unprecedented in the modern era of English football. Their final match against Leicester City epitomized their season - falling behind early but fighting back to win 2-1, with goals from Henry and Vieira.

The remarkable achievement of Arsenal's 2003-2004 unbeaten run in the Premier League was not solely the result of individual brilliance; it was underpinned by an extraordinary sense of teamwork, unwavering determination, and astute tactical acumen.

The Essence of Teamwork

Arsène Wenger's Arsenal was a symphony of coordinated team effort. Each player understood their role and the importance of their contribution to the team's success. This understanding fostered a strong sense of collective responsibility, where players seamlessly covered for one another and worked towards a common goal.

The striking partnership of Thierry Henry and Dennis Bergkamp exemplified this teamwork. Henry's pace and finishing complemented Bergkamp's vision and creativity. In midfield, Patrick Vieira and Gilberto Silva formed a formidable duo, blending physicality with technical prowess, while Robert Pires and Freddie Ljungberg provided width and attacking thrust.

Defensively, the partnership of Sol Campbell and Kolo Touré, flanked by Ashley Cole and Lauren, was robust and resilient. The defensive unit's ability to absorb pressure and launch counter-attacks was a cornerstone of Arsenal's gameplay. Jens Lehmann, in goal, provided the last line of defense with consistent and crucial saves.

Determination to Succeed

The unbeaten run was as much a mental achievement as it was physical or technical. Arsenal displayed a relentless determination to win, often finding ways to emerge victorious in the face of adversity. This determination was evident in their ability to grind out results, even when they were not playing at their best.

Games like the draw against Manchester United at Old Trafford, where Arsenal faced immense pressure, showcased the team's mental fortitude. Their ability to stay focused, maintain composure, and execute their game plan under pressure was a testament to their determination to maintain the unbeaten streak.

Tactical Acumen

Wenger's tactical acumen was a fundamental element in the success of the Invincibles. He built a team capable of adapting to different challenges, switching formations and tactics as required. Wenger's philosophy emphasized fluid, attacking football, but he also instilled a disciplined defensive structure.

Arsenal's tactical flexibility allowed them to control games through possession, but they were also adept at quick transitions and exploiting spaces on the counter-attack. Wenger's decision to employ players in versatile roles – like using Ljungberg and Pires as wide midfielders who could drift in and score – added a layer of unpredictability to their play.

A Culture of Excellence

The Invincibles season was a culmination of building a culture of excellence at Arsenal. Wenger fostered a team environment where players were encouraged to express themselves but also held accountable to the team's standards. The blend of experienced players with young, emerging talents created a dynamic team environment where learning and development were constant.

Legacy of the Invincibles

Impact on Arsenal

For Arsenal, the legacy of the Invincibles era is profound and multifaceted. It was a period that solidified the club's status as one of the elite teams in England and Europe. The unbeaten season was the pinnacle of Arsène Wenger's tenure, showcasing his visionary approach to football management and team building. This era set a benchmark for the club, a standard of excellence that future teams would aspire to.

The Invincibles' season also had a lasting impact on Arsenal's fan culture and global brand. It attracted a new generation of fans, drawn to the team's style of play and the charismatic personalities within the squad. The achievement contributed significantly to Arsenal's global appeal, elevating the club's status and marketability worldwide.

Influence on the Premier League

In the Premier League, the legacy of the Invincibles is indelible. They set a new bar for success, challenging other clubs to elevate their standards. The unbeaten run sparked a shift in the competitive landscape of the Premier League, prompting rival clubs to invest more in player acquisitions, youth development, and managerial appointments to challenge Arsenal's dominance.

The tactical sophistication and style of play exhibited by the Invincibles also influenced the tactical evolution of the Premier League. Wenger's approach, emphasizing skillful, attacking football and the importance of a solid defensive foundation, inspired other teams and managers to adopt similar philosophies. This shift contributed to the Premier League's reputation as not just a physically demanding league but also one rich in technical and tactical prowess.

Changing Footballing Philosophies

The success of the Invincibles had broader implications for footballing philosophy. Wenger's belief in nurturing talent, focusing on player health and nutrition, and employing a more analytical approach to the game influenced football management and coaching strategies globally.

The Invincibles demonstrated the effectiveness of building a team that balanced technical skill with physical strength, combined with a strong team ethos and mental resilience. This approach challenged traditional footballing philosophies, which often emphasized physicality over skill or vice versa.

Legacy of Excellence and Perfection

The unbeaten record of the Invincibles stands as a symbol of excellence and perfection in football. It represents an ideal that teams and players strive for – not just winning, but doing so with style, grace, and an undefeated record. The legacy of the Invincibles is not just in the record books but in the idea that football at its best is an art form, a spectacle that combines athletic excellence with tactical intelligence and creative expression.

1999 Women's World Cup Triumph

Team Background

The 1999 Women's World Cup, hosted by the United States, remains one of the most significant events in the history of women's soccer. The triumph of the U.S. Women's National Team (USWNT) in this tournament was a watershed moment, not only due to their victory but also for the impact it had on the popularity and recognition of women's soccer globally. The team's journey to World Cup glory was paved with talent, determination, and a collective spirit that captured the imagination of fans worldwide.

Team Composition and Key Players

The 1999 USWNT was a blend of experienced veterans and talented newcomers, creating a dynamic and formidable team. Central to this squad were several key players, each bringing their unique skills and leadership qualities to the team.

• Mia Hamm: Already a prominent figure in women's soccer, Mia Hamm was one of the world's best players at the time. Known for her exceptional speed, skill, and scoring ability, Hamm was a critical offensive force for the team.

• Julie Foudy: As a midfielder and co-captain, Foudy was known for her leadership on and off the field. Her ability to control the midfield and her tireless work rate were crucial to the team's performance.

• Brandi Chastain: A versatile player known for her defensive prowess, Chastain would also play a pivotal role in one of the tournament's most iconic moments.

• Kristine Lilly: An incredibly versatile player, Lilly's experience and consistency were vital to the team.

• Michelle Akers: A veteran of the team, Akers' presence in the midfield was a significant advantage for the U.S. Her physical and commanding play style set the tone for the team's performances.

• Briana Scurry: The goalkeeper's remarkable skills were a cornerstone of the team's defense. Her performance, especially in the final, was instrumental in the team's success.

Road to the World Cup

The USWNT entered the 1999 World Cup as one of the favorites, having won the inaugural tournament in 1991 and finished third in 1995. The team's preparation for the 1999 tournament was intense, with a focus on both physical and technical aspects of the game. The players were also acutely aware of the potential impact of the World Cup being hosted on home soil and the opportunity to grow the sport in the U.S.

In the lead-up to the World Cup, the USWNT engaged in a rigorous schedule of training camps and international matches. This preparation was part of a broader strategy to not only hone their skills but also to increase the visibility of the team and build excitement for the tournament. The players were involved in promotional activities, which helped to draw public attention and boost attendance for the upcoming games.

Group Stage and Knockout Rounds

The USWNT's performance in the group stage of the tournament was dominant. They won all three of their group matches, against Denmark, Nigeria, and North Korea, showcasing their offensive power and defensive solidity. In the knockout rounds, they continued their impressive form, defeating Germany in the quarterfinals and Brazil in the semifinals. These victories set the stage for a final against China, which would become one of the most memorable matches in the history of women's soccer.

The road to the 1999 Women's World Cup was a journey of hard work, strategic preparation, and a growing sense of the potential impact of their success. The team's blend of skill, experience, and unity, combined with the increasing public interest in women's soccer, set the stage for a tournament that would not only crown them as champions but also change the landscape of women's sports forever.

The Tournament

Group Stage

USA vs Denmark (3-0): The USWNT opened their World Cup campaign with a convincing win against Denmark. The team showcased their offensive prowess, with goals from Mia Hamm, Julie Foudy, and Kristine Lilly. The victory set a positive tone for the tournament, demonstrating the team's preparedness and skill.

USA vs Nigeria (7-1): In their second group match, the U.S. team faced Nigeria. The game turned out to be a goal fest for the USWNT, highlighting their dominant attacking capabilities. Michelle Akers and Cindy Parlow scored two goals each, while Mia Hamm, Tiffeny Milbrett, and Brandi Chastain each added one. The U.S. team's overwhelming victory underscored their status as tournament favorites.

USA vs North Korea (3-0): Completing the group stage with a perfect record, the U.S. team comfortably defeated North Korea. Goals from

Tiffeny Milbrett, Shannon MacMillan, and Tisha Venturini showcased the depth and versatility of the U.S. attack. The defense, led by goalkeeper Briana Scurry, remained solid, keeping another clean sheet.

Quarterfinal

USA vs Germany (3-2): The quarterfinal against Germany was a fiercely contested match, highlighting the USWNT's resilience under pressure. Brandi Chastain opened the scoring with an own goal, giving Germany an early lead. However, the U.S. team responded emphatically with goals from Joy Fawcett, Tiffeny Milbrett, and Brandi Chastain. The match was a testament to the team's mental toughness and ability to come back from behind.

Semifinal

USA vs Brazil (2-0): Facing Brazil in the semifinals, the USWNT delivered a commanding performance. Cindy Parlow and Michelle Akers scored, ensuring a comfortable win and a place in the final. The U.S. team's defense was particularly notable, neutralizing Brazil's renowned attacking threats.

The Final

The final of the 1999 Women's World Cup, held on July 10th at the Rose Bowl in Pasadena, California, was not just a soccer match; it was a cultural and sporting milestone. The U.S. Women's National Team (USWNT) faced off against China in a game that would become one of the most iconic in the history of women's sports.

The Atmosphere

The Rose Bowl was packed with over 90,000 spectators, evidence of the growing popularity of women's soccer in the United States and worldwide. The crowd was a sea of American flags and enthusiastic fans, creating an electrifying atmosphere that underscored the significance of the occasion.

Regulation Time and Extra Time

The match itself was a tense and tightly contested affair. Both teams were well-organized, displaying tactical discipline and skill. The USWNT, led by coach Tony DiCicco, faced a formidable Chinese team known for its technical ability and strategic play.

Throughout the game, both teams created scoring opportunities but were unable to convert them into goals. The U.S. had several chances, with Mia Hamm, Kristine Lilly, and Cindy Parlow leading the attack, but the Chinese defense, along with their goalkeeper Gao Hong, remained resilient. Similarly, the U.S. defense, anchored by players like Carla Overbeck, Joy Fawcett, and Brandi Chastain, alongside goalkeeper Briana Scurry, effectively neutralized China's offensive threats.

As regulation time ended with the score still 0-0, the game moved into extra time. The tension increased as both teams vied for the winning goal, but neither could break the deadlock, sending the match into a penalty shootout – a fitting climax to a closely contested World Cup final.

The Penalty Shootout

The penalty shootout was a dramatic and nerve-wracking conclusion to the tournament. China shot first, with Carla Overbeck stepping up for the first U.S. penalty and confidently scoring. The next few penalties saw both teams converting their shots with precision. However, the pivotal moment came when Briana Scurry made a crucial save against China's third penalty taker, Liu Ying. Scurry's save, a combination of anticipation and athleticism, shifted the momentum in favor of the U.S.

With the U.S. leading 4-3 and needing only one more goal to win, Brandi Chastain stepped up to take the fifth and potentially final penalty for the U.S. team. In what would become one of the most memorable moments in sports history, Chastain struck the ball with power and accuracy into the top corner of the net, clinching victory for the U.S. team.

Chastain's iconic celebration – falling to her knees and ripping off her jersey – captured the joy, relief, and triumphant spirit of the moment. It was a spontaneous and genuine display of emotion that symbolized the liberation and empowerment that this victory represented for women in sports.

Legacy of the Final

The 1999 Women's World Cup final, especially the penalty shootout, was more than just a crowning achievement in sports. It was a cultural phenomenon that broke barriers and challenged perceptions about women's soccer and women's sports in general. The image of the USWNT celebrating their victory became a symbol of female athleticism and empowerment.

Impact and Legacy

The 1999 Women's World Cup victory by the U.S. Women's National Team (USWNT) was more than a triumph in sports; it was a watershed moment that left an enduring legacy on the cultural and social landscape, both in the United States and globally. This victory transcended the realm of soccer, sparking changes in the perception of women's sports and empowering a new generation of female athletes.

Cultural Impact in the United States

In the United States, the 1999 World Cup triumph marked a significant breakthrough in the cultural acceptance and popularity of women's soccer and women's sports in general. The tournament, especially the final in Pasadena, was a showcase of women's sports at its best. It drew unprecedented media attention and public interest, shattering attendance and television viewing records.

The iconic image of Brandi Chastain celebrating her winning penalty kick became a symbol of female strength, determination, and empowerment. It challenged traditional stereotypes of femininity and athleticism, portraying women athletes in a new light. This image, and the victory as a whole, inspired countless young girls to participate in sports, leading to a surge in female participation in soccer and other athletic activities across the nation.

The success of the USWNT also had a significant impact on the infrastructure and funding of women's sports in the U.S. It led to increased investment in women's soccer at both the grassroots and professional levels. The establishment and growth of professional women's soccer leagues in the U.S., such as the Women's United Soccer Association (WUSA) and later the National Women's Soccer League (NWSL), can be partly attributed to the increased interest and visibility generated by the 1999 World Cup.

Social and Global Impact

Globally, the 1999 World Cup served as a catalyst for the growth of women's soccer. It demonstrated that women's sports could attract large audiences and generate significant commercial interest. This realization spurred increased investment and development in women's soccer programs worldwide, leading to higher competitive standards and greater opportunities for female athletes.

The victory also played a role in challenging gender norms in sports. It provided a platform to address issues of gender inequality in athletics, such as disparities in pay, resources, and media coverage between men's and women's sports. The success and visibility of the USWNT brought these issues to the forefront, sparking conversations and actions towards greater equity in sports.

Legacy of Empowerment and Inspiration

The legacy of the 1999 World Cup victory is multifaceted. It changed the landscape of women's sports, breaking down barriers and paving the way for future generations of female athletes. The tournament and particularly the U.S. team's triumph, served as a powerful example of the potential and impact of women in sports.

Two decades later, the impact of this victory is still evident. It continues to inspire young athletes, influence sports policies, and shape cultural attitudes towards women's sports. The 1999 Women's World Cup stands as a testament to the power of sports to effect social change and empower individuals, setting a standard for how sports can be a force for positive societal impact.

The Fair Play of Aaron Mokoena

Early Career and Becoming the Youngest National Player

Aaron Mokoena's journey in professional soccer is a remarkable tale of talent, dedication, and a historic ascent to national recognition. Known for his fair play and leadership on the field, Mokoena's early career laid the foundation for his status as a South African football icon and his record as the youngest player to represent the national team.

Early Life and Introduction to Football

Aaron Mokoena was born on November 25, 1980, in Boipatong, South Africa. Growing up during a transformative period in the nation's history, Mokoena found solace and passion in football. This sport, deeply ingrained in the cultural fabric of South Africa, became a significant part of his life from a young age. Mokoena's early exposure to soccer in the streets and local fields of Boipatong was the beginning of a journey that would see him ascend to the pinnacle of South African football.

Rising Through the Ranks

Mokoena's talent was evident early on. He possessed a natural understanding of the game, coupled with a physical presence that was rare for his age. His journey in professional soccer began when he joined the Jomo Cosmos youth academy, a renowned breeding ground for South African football talent. Under the guidance of Jomo Sono, a South African football legend, Mokoena honed his skills and developed an understanding of the game that belied his years.

At Jomo Cosmos, Mokoena's potential quickly became apparent. He progressed through the ranks, demonstrating a level of maturity and skill that set him apart from his peers. His performances in the youth teams caught the attention of the club's senior management and soon after, the national team selectors.

Becoming the Youngest National Player

Mokoenas ascent to the national team was meteoric. At the age of just 18, he made his debut for the South African national team, Bafana Bafana, in 1999. This achievement set a record, making him the youngest player ever to represent South Africa at the senior level – a record that still stands. His debut was more than just a personal milestone; it was a moment of national significance, symbolizing the emergence of a new talent in South African football.

His early appearances for Bafana Bafana showcased his versatility as a player. Initially playing as a midfielder, Mokoena displayed a robust defensive ability, tactical intelligence, and leadership qualities that were rare in players of his age. His composure on the ball, combined with his physicality and reading of the game, made him an integral part of the national team.

Building a Reputation for Fair Play

From the outset of his career, Mokoena was noted for his fair play. He approached the game with a sense of respect for his opponents and the rules, earning him the admiration of teammates and rivals alike. This attitude towards the game, coupled with his footballing abilities,

set the foundation for a career that would be defined by leadership and integrity.

Aaron Mokoena's early career is a story of a young talent rising to meet the challenges of professional football with remarkable grace and skill. His record as the youngest player to represent South Africa stands as proof of his extraordinary ability and hard work. More than that, it marked the beginning of a career that would see him not only succeed on the field but also become a role model for fair play and sportsmanship in South African football.

Club Career and Leadership Roles

Early Club Career and Move to Europe

Mokoena's professional club career began at Jomo Cosmos, where his talent quickly became evident. His performances in the South African league garnered attention from European clubs, paving the way for his move to Bayer Leverkusen in Germany in 1999. Although he did not make a first-team appearance for Leverkusen, this move was key in exposing him to European football's competitive nature.

Loan to Ajax and Development in the Netherlands

Mokoena's career took a significant turn when he was loaned to Ajax, one of the Netherlands' most prestigious clubs. At Ajax, he gained valuable experience and exposure to high-level football. His time in the Eredivisie was marked by growth and development, both as a player and a leader. Mokoena's physical style of play, coupled with his tactical understanding, made him a valuable asset to the team.

Move to Belgium and England

Following his stint in the Netherlands, Mokoena moved to Belgium to play for Germinal Beerschot. It was here that his leadership qualities began to shine through more prominently. He became known for his commanding presence on the field and his ability to organize and motivate his teammates.

Mokoena's leadership and defensive skills caught the attention of English club Blackburn Rovers, where he moved in 2005. In the English Premier League, one of the world's most challenging football leagues, Mokoena's qualities were put to the test. He rose to the challenge admirably, becoming a key player for Blackburn. Known for his tough tackling and no-nonsense defending, he earned the nickname "The Axe."

At Blackburn, Mokoena's leadership on the field was evident. He was a player who led by example, displaying a high level of professionalism, commitment, and a never-say-die attitude. His tenure at Blackburn solidified his reputation as a reliable and formidable defensive midfielder and central defender.

Later Career and Continued Leadership

Mokoena continued to demonstrate his leadership qualities when he moved to Portsmouth in 2009. Even as the club faced financial difficulties and relegation, Mokoena's character and leadership never waned. He was a stabilizing presence in the team, often lifting the spirits of his teammates and leading by example during challenging times.

After his time in England, Mokoena returned to South Africa, where he played for Bidvest Wits. His return was not just a homecoming but also an opportunity to impart his experience and knowledge to the younger generation of South African footballers.

Off-Field Leadership and Philanthropy

Mokoena's leadership extended beyond the football field. He was deeply involved in charity work and used his platform to promote various social causes. The Aaron Mokoena Foundation, which he established, is a testament to his commitment to giving back to the community and supporting youth development through sport and education.

Advocacy for Fair Play and Sportsmanship

Embodiment of Fair Play

Mokoena's approach to the game has always been characterized by a deep respect for both the rules and the spirit of soccer. Known for his tough but fair defensive play, he earned respect from teammates, opponents, and officials alike. Mokoena understood that respect for the game and its participants was paramount, and he consistently demonstrated this through his actions on the field. His ability to maintain composure in high-stakes situations and refrain from retaliatory behavior in the face of provocation set him apart as a model professional.

Promoting Sportsmanship

Mokoena's influence in promoting sportsmanship was most evident in his interactions with fellow players, especially younger teammates. He often took on a mentorship role, guiding emerging players on how to conduct themselves professionally. Mokoena's lessons went beyond technical and tactical advice, focusing also on the importance of playing with integrity, respecting opponents, and upholding the values of the sport.

His leadership extended to his role as the captain of the South African national team, Bafana Bafana. In this capacity, he was not just a tactical leader but also a moral compass for the team. He led by example, instilling a culture of fair play and mutual respect within the squad. His tenure as captain was marked by a noticeable ethos of sportsmanship that resonated with both his teammates and the broader soccer community.

Influence on Younger Players

Mokoena's impact on younger players cannot be overstated. Through his foundation and various youth initiatives, he has actively worked to instill the values of fair play and sportsmanship in the next generation of soccer players. His engagement in youth development programs has provided a platform for him to impart the principles of respect, integrity, and professionalism to young aspiring athletes.

His involvement in these programs often goes beyond mere coaching, focusing on developing the character of young players. Mokoena emphasizes the importance of discipline, respect for opponents and officials, and the role of sportsmanship in personal and athletic development.

Legacy in Soccer

The legacy Aaron Mokoena leaves in soccer is multifaceted. While his achievements on the field are commendable, his advocacy for fair play and sportsmanship is perhaps even more significant. He has been a powerful advocate for playing the game in the right spirit, and his influence has helped shape the attitudes of countless players.

In a sport where competitive pressure can sometimes lead to unsporting behavior, Mokoena's career stands as a beacon of how to compete fiercely yet fairly. His dedication to upholding the highest standards of sportsmanship has earned him immense respect and serves as a model for players at all levels of the sport.

Aaron Mokoena's commitment to fair play and sportsmanship is a defining aspect of his career and legacy. His efforts to promote these values in soccer have contributed significantly to the sport, influencing not just the current generation of players but also shaping the attitudes of future soccer stars. Mokoena's legacy is a reminder that success in soccer is not only measured by victories and accolades but also by the respect and integrity one brings to the game.

Legacy in South African Football

Aaron Mokoena's legacy in South African football is profound and enduring, marked not only by his exceptional performances on the field but also by his significant contributions to the development of the sport in the country. As a national team captain and a role model,

Mokoena has left an indelible mark on South African soccer, influencing generations of players and fans.

Impact on the National Team

Mokoena's impact on the South African national team, Bafana Bafana, has been monumental. His record as the youngest player ever to be capped by the national team is just the tip of the iceberg in terms of his contributions. Mokoena earned over 100 caps for South Africa, a testament to his longevity, consistency, and importance to the team.

As captain, Mokoena led Bafana Bafana with distinction, particularly during a period that included their participation in the 2010 FIFA World Cup, the first ever held on African soil. His leadership during the World Cup was crucial, not only in terms of his performances on the field but also in how he carried the hopes and expectations of the nation. He was a unifying figure, embodying the spirit of South Africa during a pivotal moment in the country's footballing history.

Mokoena's influence extended beyond leading the team in matches. He played a vital role in the dressing room, mentoring younger players and instilling a professional work ethic. His experience in European football provided valuable insights that he shared with his teammates, helping to elevate the overall standard of the national team.

Contributions to Football Development

Beyond his contributions on the pitch, Mokoena has been instrumental in the development of football in South Africa. His involvement in youth development initiatives has been particularly impactful. Through the Aaron Mokoena Foundation and various outreach programs, he has worked to provide opportunities for young players to learn and grow in the sport.

Mokoena's efforts have focused on not just developing football skills but also on using the sport as a tool for social development. He has been an advocate for using football to teach life skills, promote education, and provide pathways for young South Africans to build a better future. His commitment to these causes demonstrates a deep understanding of the role of sports in society and a desire to give back to the community that supported his journey.

Role Model and Ambassador

Mokoena's status as a role model and ambassador for South African football cannot be overstated. His professional demeanor, commitment to fair play, and success on the international stage have made him an icon in South African sports. He represents the potential of South African athletes to succeed globally while maintaining a strong connection to their roots.

His journey from the streets of Boipatong to the world stage provides inspiration to countless young South Africans. Mokoena has shown that with talent, hard work, and dedication, it is possible to reach the highest levels of the sport.

Hope Solo's Goalkeeping Excellence

Early Life and Career Start

Hope Amelia Solo was born on July 30, 1981, in Richland, Washington. Growing up in a sports-oriented family, Solo was introduced to soccer at a young age. Her athleticism was evident early on, and she showed a natural affinity for sports. Solo's introduction to soccer was more than just the start of a sporting career; it was the beginning of a lifelong passion.

From the outset, Solo displayed remarkable talent and a competitive drive. She played soccer with boys in her neighborhood, honing her skills and toughness. This early exposure to a higher level of physicality and competition laid the groundwork for her future success in the sport.

High School Stardom and Versatility

During her high school years, Solo's soccer talent truly began to shine. She attended Richland High School, where she quickly made a name for herself as a forward, displaying impressive goal-scoring abilities. Her prowess on the field was not limited to scoring goals; she also exhibited a keen understanding of the game and exceptional athleticism, two qualities that would later define her goalkeeping career.

Despite her success as a forward, Solo's transition to goalkeeping was a pivotal moment in her soccer journey. The shift to goalkeeper was initially a tactical decision by her high school coach, but it quickly became apparent that Solo had found her true calling on the soccer field.

Collegiate Success and Positional Shift

Solo's transition to goalkeeping was solidified during her time at the University of Washington. Playing for the Washington Huskies, she embraced her role as a goalkeeper and began to develop the skills that would make her one of the best in the world. Her time in college was marked by intense training and a deepening understanding of the intricacies of goalkeeping.

At the University of Washington, Solo's talent as a goalkeeper flourished. She set numerous records and received several honors, showcasing her ability to make crucial saves and command her penalty area. Her agility, quick reflexes, and fearless approach to stopping shots became hallmarks of her playing style.

Early National Team Experience

Solo's exceptional performances in college did not go unnoticed. She was called up to the U.S. Women's National Team, where she began her international career. This was a significant step for Solo, providing her with an opportunity to compete against the best players in the world and further refine her goalkeeping skills.

Solo's early life and transition to becoming a goalkeeper paint the picture of an athlete who was not only immensely talented but also adaptable and determined. Her journey from a goal-scoring forward to one of the most formidable goalkeepers in women's soccer is a testament to her hard work, resilience, and unwavering dedication to the sport. Solo's early career laid a strong foundation for what would become a legendary presence in the world of soccer, marked by exceptional performances, numerous accolades, and a lasting impact on the game.

Rise to Stardom

Collegiate Soccer and Record-Breaking Performances

Hope Solo's collegiate career at the University of Washington set the stage for her future success. From 1999 to 2002, she was the backbone of the Huskies' soccer team, showcasing her exceptional goalkeeping skills. Solo left a lasting legacy at the university, setting records for the most shutouts, saves, and lowest goals-against average.

During her time in college, Solo developed a reputation for her agility, commanding presence in goal, and an uncanny ability to make game-changing saves. Her performances did not go unnoticed, and she quickly garnered attention as one of the most promising goalkeeping talents in the country.

Entry into the U.S. Women's National Team

Solo's entry into the U.S. Women's National Team marked the beginning of an illustrious international career. She was first called up to the national team in 2000, an acknowledgment of her growing reputation as a top goalkeeper. However, her journey with the national team was not without challenges. She had to compete against well-established goalkeepers, a demonstration of the depth and competitiveness of the U.S. squad.

Over the next few years, Solo worked tirelessly to improve her skills and establish herself within the team. Her dedication to training understanding of the game, and physical fitness were key factors in her ascent. She gradually became a regular feature in the national team, showcasing her ability to perform at the highest level.

Establishing Dominance in International Soccer

Solo's breakthrough as a dominant force in international soccer came in the mid-2000s. By then, she had established herself as the first-choice goalkeeper for the U.S. Women's National Team. Her performances in major tournaments were a clear indication of her world-class abilities.

In the 2007 FIFA Women's World Cup, Solo's skills were on full display. Her outstanding performances helped the team reach the semi-finals, where they faced a strong Brazilian side. Despite the team's eventual defeat, Solo's individual performances were highly praised.

2008 Olympic Redemption and Rise to Fame

The 2008 Beijing Olympics was a turning point for Solo. She played a crucial role in the U.S. team's journey to the gold medal, making key saves throughout the tournament, including in the final against Brazil. This victory was not just a redemption for the 2007 World Cup disappointment but also cemented Solo's status as one of the leading goalkeepers in women's soccer.

Continued Excellence and Record-Setting Career

Solo continued to excel in her role with the U.S. team in the following years. She was instrumental in the U.S. team's second-place finish in the 2011 FIFA Women's World Cup and their gold medal win at the 2012 London Olympics. Her performances in these tournaments were marked by resilience, technical excellence, and an unwavering competitive spirit.

Her ability to perform under pressure, combined with her exceptional skill set, set her apart. Solo set numerous records with the national team, including the most clean sheets, which is a testament to her consistency and longevity at the highest level of the game.

Key Performances and Resilience

2007 FIFA Women's World Cup

One of Solo's early defining moments on the international stage came during the 2007 FIFA Women's World Cup. Despite the team's ultimate disappointment in not winning the tournament, Solo's performances in the earlier rounds were pivotal. Her excellent shot-stopping ability and command of the penalty area were crucial in the USA's progress to the semi-finals. The tournament was also significant for Solo personally, as she faced both professional and personal challenges, demonstrating her mental toughness and resilience.

2008 Beijing Olympics – A Story of Redemption

The 2008 Beijing Olympics was a redemption arc for Solo. After the controversy and disappointment of the 2007 World Cup, Solo returned to the international stage with a point to prove. She was instrumental in the USA's gold medal victory, showcasing exceptional goalkeeping skills throughout the tournament. In the final against Brazil, Solo made several key saves, including a critical stop against Brazilian forward Marta, ensuring a 1-0 victory for the USA. This performance not only solidified her reputation as a top goalkeeper but also exemplified her ability to overcome adversity and succeed.

2011 FIFA Women's World Cup

The 2011 World Cup in Germany was another highlight in Solo's career. She played a key role in the USA's run to the final. Her standout performance came in the quarter-final match against Brazil. Solo saved a penalty in extra time, a pivotal moment that kept the USA in the game, which they eventually won on penalties. Throughout the tournament, Solo's leadership and skill were evident, earning her the Golden Glove award for the best goalkeeper of the tournament.

2012 London Olympics

Continuing her string of impressive performances, the 2012 Olympics in London saw Solo once again playing a key role in the USA's gold medal victory. She made several key saves throughout the tournament, particularly in the final against Japan. Her consistency and ability to perform under pressure were vital in securing back-to-back Olympic gold medals for the USA.

Resilience in Facing Challenges

Hope Solo's career has been as much about resilience as it has been about success. She faced numerous challenges, both on and off the field, but consistently demonstrated the mental fortitude to overcome them. Whether dealing with injuries, controversies, or high-pressure situations in major tournaments, Solo's resilience and determination were unwavering.

Legacy and Influence

Hope Solo's remarkable career extends beyond her exceptional performances as a goalkeeper. Her impact on women's soccer, advocacy for gender equality in sports, and status as a role model for young female athletes constitute a legacy that is as profound as it is influential.

Impact on Women's Soccer

Solo has indelibly shaped the landscape of women's soccer, particularly in the realm of goalkeeping. Her athleticism, technical skill, and mental toughness redefined the standards for female goalkeepers. She brought a level of professionalism and dedication to the role that inspired both her teammates and competitors to elevate their own performances. Solo's style of play – aggressive, commanding, and technically sound – set a new benchmark in women's soccer, inspiring a generation of young goalkeepers.

Through her career, Solo also contributed to raising the profile of women's soccer globally. Her performances in World Cups and Olympic Games brought attention to the sport, showcasing the high level of competition and skill present in women's soccer. This visibility was crucial in increasing the sport's popularity and encouraging investment in women's soccer programs worldwide.

Advocacy for Gender Equality

Solo has been a vocal advocate for gender equality in sports. She has consistently used her platform to speak out against disparities in pay, treatment, and conditions between men's and women's soccer. Her willingness to address these issues publicly brought them to the forefront of conversations in the sports world, challenging governing bodies and the wider sports community to take action.

Her legal battle against the United States Soccer Federation over equal pay was a landmark moment in the fight for gender equality in sports. By taking a stand, Solo, along with her teammates, highlighted the systemic issues facing female athletes and ignited a global conversation about equity in sports.

Influence as a Role Model

Solo's journey from a small town in Washington to the pinnacle of international soccer serves as a powerful example for young athletes, especially girls and young women. Her resilience in overcoming personal and professional challenges resonates with many who face their own obstacles in pursuing their sporting ambitions.

Solo's dedication to her craft, her commitment to excellence, and her ability to perform under pressure make her a role model for aspiring goalkeepers and players. Her career demonstrates that with hard work, determination, and a strong belief in oneself, it is possible to achieve greatness.

Moreover, Solo's advocacy work off the field adds another layer to her role model status. Her fight for equality and justice in sports has inspired female athletes to stand up for their rights and has encouraged a new generation to not only aspire to be great athletes but also to be advocates for change.

Sunil Chhetri's Impact in Indian Football

Early Career and Rise in Indian Football

Born on August 3, 1984, in Secunderabad, India, Sunil Chhetri's introduction to football was influenced by his family's sporting background. His father, KB Chhetri, was an officer in the Indian Army and played football, while his mother and her twin sister played for the Nepal women's national team. This familial connection to the sport was instrumental in nurturing his early interest in football.

Growing up, Chhetri was exposed to various sporting disciplines, but his passion for football quickly became apparent. He honed his skills in local tournaments and school competitions, displaying a natural aptitude for the game. His early years were marked by a dedication to improving his technical skills and understanding of football, laying the foundation for his future success.

Start of Professional Career in India

Chhetri's professional career began with Mohun Bagan, one of India's most prestigious clubs, in 2002. This was a significant step for the young Chhetri, as it offered him a platform to showcase his talent on a larger stage. At Mohun Bagan, he quickly made an impression with his agility, skillful ball control, and knack for finding the back of the net.

After Mohun Bagan, Chhetri moved to JCT Mills, where he further honed his skills and emerged as a promising talent in Indian football. His time at JCT was crucial in his development as a player, as he became more consistent in his performances and started to attract attention from the national selectors.

Rise to National Prominence

Chhetri's national career took off when he made his debut for the Indian national team in 2005. He immediately made an impact with his performance, showcasing his ability to play under pressure and his natural goal-scoring instincts. Chhetri's emergence as a key player for the national team was a sign of changing times in Indian football which was yearning for a new hero.

In the following years, Chhetri's contributions to the national team were pivotal. He played a key role in India's triumphs in the Nehru Cup, the SAFF Championship, and their impressive performances in the AFC Asian Cup. His leadership and ability to perform in crucial matches elevated his status to that of a national icon.

Chhetri's Role in a Cricket-Dominated Country

In a country where cricket is almost a religion, Chhetri's rise in football is a reflection of his exceptional talent and hard work. He became the face of Indian football, inspiring a new generation of players and fans in a nation where football had long been overshadowed by cricket.

Chhetri's journey in Indian football has not just been about personal accolades; it has been about inspiring a nation to embrace the beautiful game. His commitment to the sport and his performances for the national team have played a significant role in increasing football's popularity in India.

Club Success and International Exploits

Club Achievements in India and Abroad

Chhetri's club career in India has been characterized by success and accolades. After his initial stints with Mohun Bagan and JCT Mills, where he emerged as a promising talent, Chhetri moved to East Bengal, one of India's top clubs. At East Bengal, he continued to showcase his goal-scoring abilities, becoming a fan favorite due to his consistent performances.

One of the highlights of Chhetri's club career was his time with Bengaluru FC, a club he joined in 2013. At Bengaluru FC, Chhetri became an integral part of the team's success. He led the club to its first-ever I-League title in the 2013-2014 season and followed it up with another title in 2015-2016. His leadership, coupled with his prolific scoring, played a significant role in Bengaluru FC's rise in Indian football.

Chhetri's foray into international club football added another dimension to his career. He had stints with Kansas City Wizards (now Sporting Kansas City) in Major League Soccer (MLS) and Sporting Clube de Portugal's reserve side. Although these stints were brief, they were significant in terms of the experience and exposure they provided. Playing in MLS and the Portuguese league helped Chhetri gain insights into different styles of play and footballing cultures, which enriched his overall game.

Impact and Leadership in the Indian National Team

Chhetri's contributions to the Indian national team have been monumental. He has been a key player for India since making his debut and quickly became the team's captain, a role in which he thrived. His leadership on and off the field has been inspirational for both his teammates and young aspiring footballers across the nation.

Under his captaincy, the Indian team achieved notable successes. Chhetri was instrumental in India's victories in the Nehru Cup (2007, 2009, 2012) and the SAFF Championship (2011). He also played a crucial role in India's campaign in the 2011 AFC Asian Cup, where the team made its first appearance in the tournament after a gap of 27 years.

Record-Breaking Goal-Scoring Feats

Chhetri's goal-scoring record for the national team is exceptional. He has consistently been the top scorer for India, breaking records and earning accolades. His ability to find the back of the net in decisive matches has not only helped India clinch important wins but has also endeared him to fans across the country.

Role as a Promoter of Football in India

Advocate for Football in a Cricket-Dominated Nation

In India, where cricket is more than just a sport, Chhetri's rise as a football icon has been instrumental in drawing attention to football. He has been a vocal advocate for the sport, consistently emphasizing its potential and the need for greater investment and infrastructure development. Chhetri's passion for football is evident not only in his words but also in his actions – he has been actively involved in various initiatives aimed at promoting the sport across the country.

His influence was notably highlighted in a heartfelt appeal he made via social media, urging fans to attend and support the national team's games. This appeal, sincere and emotive, resonated with millions and led to a significant increase in attendance and support for the Indian football team. It was a clear demonstration of his commitment to the growth of football in India and his ability to mobilize support for the sport.

Increasing Football's Popularity Among Youth

Chhetri's impact on the younger generation in India has been substantial. As a role model, he has inspired countless young Indians to take up football. His journey, marked by dedication and hard work, offers a blueprint for young athletes aspiring to make it in professional football.

Through various football academies and training camps, Chhetri has been directly involved in nurturing young talent. His insights and experiences are invaluable to these young players, who look up to him not just for his skills on the field but also for his professionalism and work ethic.

Mentorship and Development of Young Talent

Chhetri's mentorship extends beyond the football field. He has been a guiding figure for young footballers, offering advice on everything from technique and tactics to fitness and mental toughness. His approachable demeanor and willingness to share his knowledge have made him a beloved figure among upcoming players.

Moreover, Chhetri has been instrumental in advocating for better coaching and training facilities for young footballers in India. He recognizes that nurturing talent from a young age is fundamental for the long-term development of football in the country.

Legacy and Influence

A Pivotal Figure in Indian Football

Chhetri's impact on Indian football is significant. He emerged as a beacon of hope and excellence in a sport that struggled for recognition and support in a cricket-centric country. His consistent performances, leadership, and charisma have not only brought success to the teams he has played for but have also significantly raised the profile of football in India.

As the captain of the national team, Chhetri led by example, both on and off the field. His commitment to the sport and his country has inspired his teammates and young players alike. Under his leadership, the Indian football team achieved notable successes, which helped in instilling a sense of pride and belief in Indian football fans.

Breaking Records and Setting Standards

His legacy is also marked by his extraordinary goal-scoring ability. He has broken numerous records, including being the second-highest international goal scorer among active players, surpassing many global football legends. This achievement is not just a personal milestone but a testament to his enduring excellence and dedication to the sport.

His ability to perform consistently at the highest level has set a new standard for professional footballers in India. Chhetri's career serves as a benchmark for aspiring footballers, showcasing the levels of commitment, fitness, and skill required to succeed at the top.

Inspiring a Generation

Perhaps one of Chhetri's most significant contributions is his influence on the younger generation. He has inspired countless young Indians to pursue football, both as fans and as players. Chhetri's journey from a young talent to a national icon demonstrates the potential of Indian football and has played a crucial role in attracting more youth to the sport.

His efforts in promoting football at the grassroots level, mentoring young players, and advocating for better facilities and opportunities for the youth have contributed immensely to the development of the sport in India.

Ongoing Contributions to Football

Chhetri's contributions to Indian football extend beyond his playing career. He has been a vocal advocate for the sport, pushing for structural improvements, better league systems, and more opportunities for young players. His insights and experiences are invaluable in shaping the future strategy and policies for football development in India.

Lionel Messi's Perseverance

Early Challenges in Rosario, Argentina

Lionel Andrés Messi was born on June 24, 1987, in Rosario, Argentina, to Jorge Messi, a steel factory manager, and his wife Celia Cuccittini, who worked in a magnet manufacturing workshop. Raised in a football-loving family, Messi developed a passion for the game at a very young age. He was greatly influenced by his family, especially his maternal grandmother, Celia, who accompanied him to training and matches. Messi joined his first soccer club, Grandoli, at the age of four, where his father coached him.

The young Messi was always smaller than his peers, a trait that would become a significant challenge in his burgeoning football career. Despite his diminutive stature, his talent was undeniable. He moved to Newell's Old Boys, a local club in Rosario, at the age of eight. His skills on the pitch were extraordinary, showcasing remarkable dribbling ability, vision, and natural football intelligence. Messi was part of a local youth team nicknamed "The Machine of '87," known for their unbeatable record and incredible talent.

Battling Growth Hormone Deficiency

At the age of 10, Messi faced a major obstacle that threatened to derail his dreams of becoming a professional footballer. He was diagnosed with a growth hormone deficiency, a condition that required expensive medical treatment, including regular injections. The cost of the treatment was beyond the financial means of the Messi family.

Despite this setback, Messi's determination and passion for the game did not wane. His family was committed to finding a way to support his treatment and continue his football development. This period was one of uncertainty and hardship for Messi and his family, as they searched for solutions to ensure he could receive the necessary treatment and pursue his football aspirations.

The Move to Barcelona

Messi's talent caught the attention of FC Barcelona's scouts when he was just 13 years old. Carles Rexach, the sporting director of Barcelona at the time, saw something special in the young Argentine and was willing to take a chance on him. In a now-legendary decision Rexach offered Messi a contract written on a napkin – an agreement to bring him to Barcelona's famed youth academy, La Masia, and to cover his medical treatment.

The move to Barcelona was a life-changing moment for Messi. Uprooting his life and moving to Spain was a significant challenge particularly at such a young age. He left behind his friends, family and familiar surroundings to embark on a journey in a new country with a new language and culture. The transition was difficult; Messi was initially homesick and struggled to integrate into his new environment. However, his talent shone through. At La Masia, Messi's skills developed rapidly, and he quickly adapted to the style of play exceeding expectations at every level of the youth system.

Rise to Stardom

Early Years at La Masia

Messi's journey at La Masia, Barcelona's youth academy, began in 2000 when he was just 13 years old. Moving to a new country and adapting to a new culture was challenging, but Messi's focus remained unwaveringly on soccer. At La Masia, he found himself in an environment that prized technical skill, tactical understanding, and a deep love for the game – all elements that resonated with Messi's natural style of play.

In these formative years, Messi underwent not only physical development, courtesy of his treatment for growth hormone deficiency, but also significant soccer development. Under the tutelage of some of the best youth coaches, he honed his skills, particularly his incredible dribbling ability, close ball control, and vision on the field. Messi's growth as a player was rapid, and he quickly moved through the ranks of the youth teams.

His performances in youth matches were nothing short of phenomenal. Messi consistently played against older and physically larger opponents, yet his talent shone through. He became known for changing games single-handedly, utilizing his low center of gravity to maneuver past defenders with ease.

Breaking Records in Youth Leagues

Messi's time in Barcelona's youth teams was marked by record-breaking performances. He was not just another promising young player; he was a prodigy setting new standards in youth soccer. His goal-scoring record was particularly impressive, often scoring upwards of 40 goals in a season for various youth teams. These extraordinary feats were early indicators of the impact Messi would have on the world of soccer.

Transition to the First Team

Messi's transition to Barcelona's first team was a natural progression given his astounding performances at the youth level. His first-team debut came at the age of 16 in a friendly match against FC Porto in November 2003. This was a significant moment, marking his entry into professional soccer.

In October 2004, at just 17, Messi made his official competitive debut for Barcelona against Espanyol. This match marked his entry into the record books as the youngest player to play in an official match for Barcelona at that time. His first league goal came the following year, against Albacete, making him the youngest scorer for the club in a La Liga match.

Establishing Himself in the First Team

Messi's integration into the first team was seamless, thanks to the nurturing environment at La Masia and his extraordinary talent. Under the guidance of coaches like Frank Rijkaard and later Pep Guardiola, Messi evolved from a talented youngster to a key player for the team.

His early years in the first team were marked by dazzling performances, showcasing not just his goal-scoring ability but also his capacity to create opportunities and assist his teammates. Messi's playing style, characterized by close ball control, rapid dribbling, and an uncanny ability to find spaces in the defense, fit perfectly with Barcelona's style of play.

Messi's breakthrough season came in 2006-2007, where he scored 14 goals in 26 league games and produced numerous assists. He played a crucial role in Barcelona's domestic and European campaigns, displaying a level of maturity and skill that belied his age. It was during this season that comparisons with soccer legends like Diego Maradona began to surface, not just for his style of play but for his impact on the game.

Rising to International Acclaim

Messi's rise to stardom at Barcelona was not just about his on-field performances. He became an integral part of a team that would go on to achieve tremendous success, both in Spain and internationally. His partnership with players like Xavi Hernandez and Andrés Iniesta was pivotal in Barcelona's dominance of European soccer.

By the time he was in his early twenties, Messi had already established himself as one of the world's best players. His consistent performances, incredible skill, and ability to produce moments of magic on the soccer field had earned him international acclaim. He was not just a star at Barcelona; he was a global soccer phenomenon, drawing attention and admiration from fans and players worldwide.

Career Highlights

Barcelona Triumphs and Records

At Barcelona, Messi's career is a chronicle of unprecedented success and record-setting performances. He became the backbone of a team that dominated both Spanish and European football for over a decade. One of the key highlights was Barcelona's treble win (La Liga, Copa del Rey, and UEFA Champions League) in the 2008-2009 season, a feat they repeated in the 2014-2015 season, with Messi playing a pivotal role in both triumphs.

Messi's scoring prowess saw him breaking multiple records. He is Barcelona's all-time top scorer and holds the record for the most goals in a calendar year, netting an astonishing 91 goals in 2012. This record broke Gerd Müller's longstanding record of 85 goals in a calendar year. Messi also holds the record for the most hat-tricks in La Liga and the Champions League.

Another significant milestone has been his eight Ballon d'Or awards, the most by any player, which he won in 2009, 2010, 2011, 2012, 2015, 2019, 2021 and 2023. These awards are testament to his consistency and standing as the world's best player over different periods of his career.

Memorable Matches and Performances

Messi's career is studded with memorable matches that underscore his genius on the field. One of the most notable performances was against Real Madrid in the Champions League semi-finals in 2011, where he scored a mesmerizing solo goal, dribbling past several defenders before scoring. Another unforgettable moment was his hat-trick in the El Clásico against Real Madrid in 2007, announcing his arrival as a world-class talent.

In the 2014-2015 Champions League season, Messi produced a moment of magic against Bayern Munich in the semi-finals, leaving Jerome Boateng on the ground before chipping the ball over Manuel Neuer. These performances not only highlighted his individual brilliance but also his ability to rise to the occasion in crucial matches.

International Achievements with Argentina

On the international stage, Messi's journey with the Argentine national team has been a mix of individual brilliance and collective pursuit of glory. Despite early criticisms of his performance with the national team, Messi led Argentina to the finals of the 2014 FIFA World Cup, where they were narrowly defeated by Germany. His performance throughout the tournament earned him the Golden Ball as the tournament's best player.

One of Messi's most cherished career moments came in 2021 when he led Argentina to victory in the Copa América, his first major international trophy. His emotional response to this triumph was evidence of his deep connection with his national team and his relentless pursuit of success on the international stage.

Legacy and Influence

Messi's influence extends beyond his scoring records and individual accolades. He has redefined the perception of an ideal footballer with his unique style, combining incredible dribbling skills, vision, and playmaking abilities with prolific goal-scoring. He has been a role model for sportsmanship, consistently maintaining a high level of performance and professionalism throughout his career.

Messi's career highlights reflect a journey of extraordinary talent, unwavering dedication, and a relentless pursuit of greatness. His records and achievements with Barcelona and Argentina are testaments to his status as one of the greatest footballers of all time.

Personal Life and Legacy

Off-Field Persona

Away from the limelight of professional football, Messi is known for his reserved and humble nature. Despite his global fame, he has maintained a relatively private personal life. Messi married Antonela Roccuzzo, his childhood sweetheart, in 2017, in a ceremony that was both a celebration of their long-standing relationship and a rare glimpse into Messi's personal world. The couple has three sons, and Messi is often seen as a doting father, sharing moments with his family that portray a tender and grounded side, contrasting with his superstar status.

Messi's humility extends to his interactions with fans and in his conduct in the public eye. He is often described as unassuming and down-to-earth, qualities that endear him to fans and observers alike. This demeanor, combined with his extraordinary talent, has contributed to his widespread popularity and respect, transcending club rivalries and national loyalties.

Philanthropy and Social Responsibility

Messi's commitment to philanthropy is a significant aspect of his legacy. His dedication to charitable efforts is exemplified through the Leo Messi Foundation, established in 2007. The foundation focuses on access to education and health care for vulnerable children, reflecting Messi's deep concern for the well-being of children worldwide. It supports various projects, including the construction of schools, sports facilities, and children's hospitals, particularly in his home country, Argentina, as well as in other parts of the world.

One of the notable initiatives of his foundation is its collaboration with UNICEF, where Messi serves as a Goodwill Ambassador. Through this role, he has been involved in campaigns and projects aimed at improving the lives of children, particularly in areas affected by poverty, conflict, and disease. Messi's involvement in these efforts highlights his awareness of the global platform he possesses and his desire to use it for the betterment of society.

Influence on the Sport

Messi's influence on football is immeasurable. He has redefined what it means to be an attacking player, combining impeccable skill, vision, and consistency at the highest level of the game. His style of play, characterized by mesmerizing dribbling, acute footballing intelligence, and extraordinary goal-scoring ability, has inspired a new generation of footballers. Young players worldwide idolize him, aspiring to emulate his style and approach to the game.

Moreover, Messi has contributed to the global appeal of football. His rivalry with Cristiano Ronaldo, another footballing great of his era, has captivated fans and media, bringing heightened attention and excitement to the sport. Messi's career at Barcelona and his performances on the international stage with Argentina have contributed to the growth of football's popularity across different continents.

Legacy Beyond Football

Lionel Messi's legacy extends beyond his achievements on the football field. He embodies the ideals of sportsmanship, dedication, and humility, setting an example for athletes in all disciplines. His journey from a young boy facing significant health challenges in Rosario to becoming one of the greatest footballers in history is a story of perseverance and resilience. It is a narrative that resonates with people beyond football fans, inspiring them to overcome their challenges and pursue their dreams with dedication and humility.

Marta's Journey to Greatness

Early Years and Start in Brazil

Marta Vieira da Silva, universally known simply as Marta, is a name synonymous with excellence in women's soccer. Her journey from a small town in Brazil to becoming one of the greatest footballers of all time is a story of determination, talent, and breaking barriers in a sport traditionally dominated by men. Marta's early years laid the foundation for a career that would inspire countless young girls and redefine women's soccer.

Early Life in Dois Riachos, Brazil

Marta was born on February 19, 1986, in Dois Riachos, a small town in Alagoas, Brazil. Growing up in a modest environment, she was introduced to soccer at a young age, a sport that is deeply ingrained in Brazilian culture. Marta's passion for the game was evident from the start. She spent countless hours playing soccer, often with boys, as there were few opportunities for girls to play the sport.

Her early experiences playing with boys were formative. They honed her skills and imbued in her a sense of resilience and competitiveness that would become hallmarks of her playing style. Despite the societal norms that discouraged girls from playing soccer, Marta's love for the game was unwavering. She often faced criticism and skepticism, but these challenges only fueled her determination to succeed.

Talent Discovery and Initial Challenges

Marta's extraordinary talent did not go unnoticed for long. She stood out in local matches with her exceptional skill, agility, and understanding of the game. However, the path to professional soccer for women in Brazil at the time was fraught with obstacles. There was limited infrastructure and support for women's soccer, and the sport was largely seen as a male domain.

Despite these challenges, Marta's abilities could not be ignored. She was scouted and began playing for a local women's team, Vasco da Gama, in Rio de Janeiro. This move was a significant step in her career, offering her a platform to develop her skills further and compete at a higher level.

Early Career in Women's Soccer

At Vasco da Gama, Marta quickly established herself as a rising star. Her performances were a revelation, showcasing not only her technical prowess and scoring ability but also her ability to play with creativity and joy. Marta's style of play drew comparisons to the legends of Brazilian soccer, earning her accolades and recognition even in her teenage years.

However, the journey was not without its hardships. The lack of professional opportunities for women in soccer in Brazil at the time meant that Marta had to constantly fight for recognition and support. She navigated these challenges with a singular focus on her goals and a belief in her abilities.

Marta's move from Brazil to Europe marked the beginning of an extraordinary chapter in her career, transforming her from a national prodigy into an international soccer icon. Her journey in European football was characterized by groundbreaking performances, setting new standards in women's soccer and establishing her as one of the game's all-time greats.

Transition to European Football

Marta's transition to European football began in 2004 when she signed with Umeå IK, a top club in Sweden's Damallsvenskan. This move was a significant leap for Marta, offering her a platform to showcase her talents on a bigger stage. At Umeå IK, Marta quickly adapted to the European style of play, bringing her unique blend of skill, speed, and flair to the team.

In Sweden, Marta's impact was immediate and profound. She helped Umeå IK dominate the Damallsvenskan and make significant strides in the UEFA Women's Champions League. Her ability to change games with her individual brilliance was a key factor in Umeå's success during her tenure with the club.

Dominance in the UEFA Women's Champions League

Marta's performances in the UEFA Women's Champions League were particularly noteworthy. She played a pivotal role in Umeå's runs in the competition, including reaching the finals in 2007 and 2008. Her technical abilities, coupled with her knack for scoring crucial goals, made her a standout player in the tournament and brought her to the attention of the wider footballing world.

Move to the United States and Global Recognition

Marta's career took another significant turn when she moved to the United States to play in the Women's Professional Soccer (WPS) league. She joined Los Angeles Sol in 2009, a move that not only elevated her career but also brought global attention to women's professional soccer in the United States. In the WPS, Marta continued to display her extraordinary talents, winning the league's MVP award in her first season.

Her time in the United States further solidified her status as a global soccer star. Marta mesmerized fans with her dazzling play, helping to popularize women's soccer in a market that had great potential for growth.

World Cup and Olympic Performances

Internationally, Marta's star continued to rise through her performances with the Brazilian national team in the FIFA Women's World Cup and the Olympics. She was instrumental in Brazil's second-place finish at the 2007 FIFA Women's World Cup, where her skill and scoring ability were on full display. Marta's performance in the tournament, including a memorable goal against the United States in the semi-final, was a defining moment in her career.

In the Olympics, Marta was a key player for Brazil, leading the team to silver medals in both the 2004 Athens and 2008 Beijing Games. Her ability to perform on the biggest stages further cemented her reputation as one of the best players in women's soccer.

Marta's rise to international stardom in European and American soccer is a journey marked by groundbreaking achievements and awe-inspiring performances. Her transition from a Brazilian talent to a global soccer icon was paved with moments of brilliance, demonstrating her unparalleled skills and impact on the sport.

Marta's Global Influence

Revolutionizing Women's Soccer Globally

Marta's influence on the global stage has been transformative. Through her exceptional skills, she has shattered stereotypes and redefined the perception of women's soccer. Her ability to combine technical prowess with unparalleled creativity and flair has brought a new level of excitement and respect to the women's game. Marta's performances in major tournaments, such as the FIFA Women's World Cup and the Olympics, have consistently showcased the high quality of women's soccer, challenging the notion that it is secondary to the men's game.

Her international success has not only brought her individual accolades but has also put a spotlight on women's soccer, increasing its popularity and visibility. Marta has been a driving force in pushing for more coverage, better infrastructure, and increased investment in women's soccer across the globe.

Advocacy for Gender Equality

Marta has been a vocal advocate for gender equality in soccer. She has used her platform to speak out against the disparities in pay, resources, and opportunities between men's and women's soccer. Her outspoken stance has brought attention to these issues, sparking dialogue and action towards creating a more equitable environment for female soccer players worldwide.

Marta as a Role Model

Perhaps Marta's most enduring impact is her status as a role model for female athletes. Her journey, marked by resilience in the face of challenges and a relentless pursuit of her dreams, serves as an inspiration to young girls worldwide. Marta has shown that with talent, determination, and hard work, it is possible to achieve greatness, regardless of the obstacles.

Her conduct on and off the field, characterized by humility, professionalism, and a genuine passion for the game, makes her an exemplary figure for aspiring soccer players. Marta's influence has encouraged countless young girls to take up soccer and pursue their athletic ambitions, fostering a new generation of players who see her as the benchmark for success in the sport.

Unprecedented FIFA World Player of the Year Titles

The cornerstone of Marta's individual accolades is her record number of FIFA World Player of the Year awards. She won this prestigious award an astonishing six times (2006, 2007, 2008, 2009, 2010, and 2018), more than any other player in the history of soccer, male or female. This achievement alone speaks volumes about her dominance, consistency, and excellence over the years. Each award was a testament to her impact on the field, as she consistently outperformed her peers with a blend of skill, agility, and footballing intelligence.

Impact in Major Tournaments

Marta's performances in major international tournaments have been nothing short of extraordinary. In the FIFA Women's World Cup, she has been a standout player, showcasing her brilliance in every edition she participated in. Her remarkable skill set, combined with her leadership qualities, has consistently placed her among the top performers.

In the 2007 Women's World Cup, Marta's prowess was on full display as she won both the Golden Ball (best player) and the Golden Boot (top scorer), leading Brazil to a second-place finish. Her tenacity and skill in the tournament were instrumental in Brazil's impressive run and highlighted her status as a world-class player.

Record-Setting Career

Marta's goal-scoring record is another testament to her legacy. She is the all-time leading scorer in FIFA Women's World Cup history with 17 goals, a remarkable achievement that underscores her longevity and prowess in front of goal. This record is not just a measure of her ability to find the back of the net but also her consistency at the highest level of international competition.

Influence Beyond Awards

While her awards and records are significant, Marta's influence transcends her on-field achievements. She has been a pivotal figure in the growth and popularization of women's soccer globally. Her presence in the sport has inspired countless young girls to pursue football, breaking down barriers and challenging gender stereotypes in sports.

Marta's professionalism, sportsmanship, and dedication to soccer have made her a beloved figure worldwide. She is revered not just for her technical skills but also for her character and the passion she brings to the game.

Legacy as a Role Model

Marta's legacy as one of the greatest female soccer players of all time is solidified not only by her achievements but also by her influential role as a model. Her journey from a modest background in Brazil to achieving global stardom is a source of inspiration. Her story is one of perseverance, resilience, and breaking barriers, making her an icon for aspiring athletes, especially girls and women in sports.

The Miracle of Leicester City (2015-2016)

Pre-Season Expectations and Team Composition

The 2015-2016 season of Leicester City FC in the English Premier League stands as one of the most remarkable underdog stories in the history of sports. At the beginning of the season, Leicester City, a team that had narrowly avoided relegation the previous season, was set against low expectations. What unfolded over the next few months was nothing short of miraculous, as this unheralded team defied odds and predictions to claim the Premier League title.

Pre-Season Expectations

Before the season started, Leicester City was considered one of the teams most likely to face relegation. They had finished the 2014-2015 season in 14th place, just six points clear of the relegation zone. The appointment of Claudio Ranieri as the new manager in July 2015 was met with skepticism. Ranieri, an experienced Italian coach, had a respectable resume but was coming off a disappointing stint with the Greece national team.

The general consensus among pundits and fans was that Leicester would struggle throughout the season. Bookmakers placed them at 5000-1 odds to win the league, a reflection of the minimal expectations surrounding the team.

Key Players and Emergence of Stars

The team composition of Leicester City was a mix of seasoned professionals, unheralded journeymen, and emerging talents. Among the standout players was Jamie Vardy, a striker who had risen through the ranks of non-league football to become a Premier League player. His pace, work rate, and goal-scoring ability would prove crucial for Leicester.

Another key figure was Riyad Mahrez, a relatively unknown winger from Algeria who possessed exceptional skill and creativity. His flair and ability to produce moments of magic were pivotal in many of Leicesters victories.

In midfield, N'Golo Kanté, a signing from French football, quickly established himself as one of the league's best defensive midfielders. His energy, ball-winning ability, and tireless running were instrumental in Leicester's style of play.

The defensive solidity was provided by the likes of Wes Morgan and Robert Huth, whose partnership at the center-back positions formed the backbone of the team. Their experience and physicality were vital in a season where Leicester's defense was tested time and again.

Kasper Schmeichel, the goalkeeper, also played a key role. His consistent performances and crucial saves kept Leicester in many close games throughout the season.

Claudio Ranieri's Leadership

Ranieri's leadership and tactical acumen were integral elements of Leicester's success. He fostered a team spirit and unity that became the envy of many bigger clubs. Ranieri's strategy often involved a counter-attacking style that utilized the pace of Vardy and Mahrez, combined with a solid and disciplined defensive setup.

His man-management skills were also fundamental. He created an environment where players felt confident and motivated, an atmosphere that played a significant role in the team outperforming all expectations.

Leicester City's pre-season expectations in the 2015-2016 season painted a picture of a team fighting for survival. However, the combination of a tactically astute manager, a group of players who rose to the occasion, and a team spirit that resonated throughout the club set the stage for one of the greatest underdog stories in football history.

The Season's Progression and Key Victories

Early Season Momentum

The season began with Leicester City quickly dispelling any notions that they would be relegation candidates. Under Claudio Ranieri's guidance, they made an unexpectedly strong start. The team showcased a remarkable ability to grind out results, with early victories setting a tone of optimism. One notable win was a 5-2 defeat to Arsenal, which, despite being a loss, displayed Leicester's potential to compete against top-tier teams.

Defining Victories and Turning Points

As the season progressed, Leicester's performances transformed from being considered flukes to genuine title contention. A significant turning point was their victory against Chelsea, the reigning champions, in December. This win not only boosted the team's confidence but also sent a clear message to their rivals about their title aspirations.

Another decisive moment came in February with a hard-fought 3-1 victory against Manchester City at the Etihad Stadium. This win was evidence of Leicester's solid defensive setup and effective counterattacking strategy. The victory

significantly bolstered their position at the top of the table and made their title challenge seem increasingly plausible.

Tactical Acumen and Team Strategy

The tactical approach implemented by Ranieri was fundamental to Leicester's success. The team played with a compact and disciplined defense, often sitting deep and absorbing pressure from opponents. The defensive solidity of Huth and Morgan, combined with Kante's tireless work in midfield, formed the bedrock of Leicester's strategy.

Offensively, the team capitalized on the pace and finishing ability of Jamie Vardy and the creativity of Riyad Mahrez. Their counter-attacking style was lethal, often catching more possession-oriented teams off guard. Vardy's record-breaking run of scoring in 11 consecutive Premier League matches was a highlight of Leicester's attacking prowess.

Overcoming Challenges and Maintaining Consistency

Leicester's ability to maintain consistency throughout the season was remarkable. They displayed not only the flair and skill needed to win matches but also the resilience to secure points in challenging situations. Their mental toughness was evident in close matches, where they managed to eke out victories or secure crucial draws.

An example of this resilience was the 2-2 draw against West Ham in April, a game in which Leicester came from behind to salvage a point despite being reduced to ten men. This match exemplified the team's fighting spirit and their unwavering determination to push for the title.

Leicester City's Unprecedented Triumph

The Final Stretch of the Season

As the season entered its final stretch, the sense of anticipation and excitement around Leicester City's title challenge grew exponentially. Each match was approached with a mix of nervous energy and determined focus, both by the players on the field and the fans in the stands and at home. The team continued to display the resilience and tactical discipline that had become their hallmark throughout the season.

Key Matches Leading to the Title

A series of critical matches in the final weeks defined Leicester City's path to glory. Crucial victories against Southampton and Sunderland, coupled with hard-fought draws against West Ham and Manchester United, edged them closer to the title. Each result was met with increasing belief that the impossible could indeed become possible.

The turning point came on May 2, 2016, in a match not involving Leicester but their closest title rivals, Tottenham Hotspur. Tottenham's draw against Chelsea meant that Leicester City, with two games still to play, were mathematically crowned Premier League champions. The result sent shockwaves through the world of football and triggered wild celebrations among Leicester City supporters and neutrals alike.

Reactions to the Triumph

The reactions to Leicester City's title win were a mix of disbelief, admiration, and joy. Fans and players alike were overwhelmed with emotion. Scenes of jubilation erupted both in Leicester and around the world, as supporters celebrated one of the greatest underdog achievements in sports history.

Manager Claudio Ranieri, who had maintained a calm and composed demeanor throughout the season, was lauded for his leadership and tactical acumen. The players, many of whom were relatively unknown or underrated before the season, became household names and were celebrated for their collective effort and team spirit.

The global football community, including fellow professionals, pundits, and rival clubs, offered their congratulations, acknowledging the magnitude of Leicester City's achievement. The victory was hailed as a victory for football, a reminder that passion, teamwork, and determination could defy the greatest of odds.

Leicester City's Unforgettable Triumph

Redefining the Competitive Landscape

Leicester City's title win had a seismic impact on the competitive landscape of English football. Traditionally dominated by clubs with substantial financial power, the Premier League was perceived as a league where success could only be bought. Leicester's triumph, achieved on a fraction of the budget of the league's traditional powerhouses, challenged this notion. It proved that strategic planning, team spirit, and a well-executed vision could compete with and overcome financial muscle.

Inspiration Beyond Football

The story of Leicester City became a source of inspiration across the globe. It resonated not just with sports fans but with anyone who appreciated the classic underdog tale. The team's journey was a demonstration of hard work, perseverance, and belief, principles that are valued in all walks of life. Their success became a motivational blueprint for other sports teams and individuals facing daunting odds in their respective fields.

Changing Perceptions in Talent Scouting

The victory also influenced the approach to talent scouting and team composition in football. Players like Jamie Vardy and Riyad Mahrez, who had been overlooked or undervalued by bigger clubs, became symbols of undiscovered or underrated talent. The success of Leicester City encouraged clubs to invest more in scouting and developing players who might not fit the traditional profile but possess immense potential.

Impact on Management and Coaching Philosophy

Claudio Ranieri's management of Leicester City offered valuable lessons in coaching philosophy. His ability to build a cohesive unit, foster a positive team environment, and effectively motivate his players was widely admired. Ranieri's approach demonstrated that empathy, humility, and adaptability were as crucial as tactical knowledge in achieving success.

Influence on Fans and the Community

The victory had a profound impact on Leicester City's fan base and the local community. It brought unprecedented global attention to the city of Leicester, fostering a deep sense of pride and unity among its residents. The triumph galvanized the club's fan base, creating a new generation of Leicester City supporters drawn by the allure of their remarkable achievement.

Legacy in Sports History

Leicester City's 2015-2016 season stands as a beacon of hope and possibility. It has secured its place as one of the most incredible underdog stories, often compared to other miraculous sporting achievements across different disciplines. The legacy of their victory is a reminder that in sports, as in life, the improbable can become reality with the right mix of determination, skill, and spirit.

Leicester City's Premier League victory in the 2015-2016 season is more than just a footballing achievement; it is a timeless story of defying the odds. The team's success had a ripple effect across English football and beyond, changing perceptions, inspiring individuals, and leaving a legacy that will be talked about for generations. In the world of sports, where fairytales are few and far between, Leicester City's triumph remains a shining example of what can be achieved against all odds.

Cristiano Ronaldo's Work Ethic

Early Years and Sporting Lisbon

Cristiano Ronaldo, one of football's most illustrious figures, is as much celebrated for his extraordinary work ethic as he is for his on-field brilliance. This relentless drive, which became the cornerstone of his career, was nurtured early in his life in Portugal and during his formative years at Sporting Lisbon.

Humble Beginnings in Madeira

Cristiano Ronaldo dos Santos Aveiro was born on February 5, 1985, in Funchal, Madeira, Portugal. Growing up in a working-class neighborhood, Ronaldo's early life was far from luxurious. His family faced financial hardships, but these challenges laid the foundation for his character – instilling a sense of determination and the importance of hard work.

From a very young age, Ronaldo showed a deep passion for football. His talent was evident, but it was his work ethic that truly set him apart. He would spend hours practicing, often skipping meals or sacrificing leisure time to hone his skills. His dedication to improving himself, even as a child, was a precursor to the discipline and commitment that would later define his professional career.

Joining Sporting Lisbon

Ronaldo's journey took a significant turn when he joined Sporting Lisbon, one of Portugal's most prestigious football academies, at the age of just 12. Moving away from his family to Lisbon was a challenging step for the young Ronaldo, but it was a sacrifice he was willing to make to pursue his dream of becoming a professional footballer.

At Sporting Lisbon, Ronaldo's work ethic intensified. He was known for being the first to arrive at training and the last to leave, constantly working on his technique, fitness, and understanding of the game. His desire to improve was relentless; he would often request extra training sessions to work on his weaknesses, showcasing an extraordinary level of dedication for someone so young.

Development of His Work Ethic

It was during his time at Sporting Lisbon that Ronaldo's work ethic began to truly develop. He recognized early on that talent alone was not enough to succeed at the highest level. His commitment to training, his focus on physical conditioning, and his determination to be the best were evident. Ronaldo was not just working hard; he was working smart, focusing on all aspects of his game.

His coaches at Sporting Lisbon were instrumental in nurturing his work ethic. They provided the guidance and structure he needed to channel his efforts effectively. Ronaldo's attitude towards training and improvement impressed everyone at the club. He was not content with being good; he wanted to be the best, and he was willing to put in the work to get there.

Early Signs of Future Greatness

Ronaldo's time at Sporting Lisbon laid the groundwork for what would become an extraordinary career. His performances for the youth teams were a glimpse of his potential, and he quickly progressed through the ranks. His debut for the Sporting Lisbon senior team at the age of 17 was a testament to his talent and hard work.

Ronaldo's early years in Portugal and his time at Sporting Lisbon were key in the development of his work ethic. From the streets of Madeira to the training grounds of Lisbon, Ronaldo's journey was marked by an unwavering commitment to excellence. This period of his life was not just about developing his skills as a footballer; it was about instilling a mindset – a relentless drive to improve, to succeed, and to defy the odds.

Success at Manchester United and Real Madrid

Manchester United: The Making of a Superstar

Ronaldo's transfer to Manchester United in 2003 was a significant moment in his career. Under the guidance of Sir Alex Ferguson, Ronaldo transformed from a talented teenager into one of the world's best footballers. His time at United was characterized by rigorous training, a relentless drive to improve, and a determination to succeed at the highest level.

During his six years at Manchester United, Ronaldo's work ethic became legendary. He was known for staying after training sessions to work on his free-kicks, improve his dribbling, and enhance his physical strength. His dedication to self-improvement was evident in his evolution as a player. He developed into a formidable goal-scorer, a master of aerial duels, and a player capable of single-handedly changing the course of games.

Ronaldo's impact at United was profound. He helped the club to three consecutive Premier League titles (2007, 2008, and 2009), the FA Cup, two League Cups, and the UEFA Champions League in 2008. Individually, he garnered numerous accolades, including the Ballon d'Or in 2008. His final season with United was particularly remarkable, where he scored 42 goals in all competitions, showcasing his transformation into one of the most lethal forwards in the game.

Real Madrid: Scaling New Heights

Ronaldo's move to Real Madrid in 2009 for a then-world record transfer fee was the start of a new chapter. At Madrid, his work ethic intensified as he strived to leave his mark in one of the world's most prestigious clubs. Ronaldo's training regime, discipline, and dedication to maintaining peak physical condition were unparalleled. He continuously worked on refining his skills, adapting his style of play, and pushing the limits of his physical abilities.

At Real Madrid, Ronaldo's goal-scoring record was nothing short of phenomenal. He became the club's all-time top scorer in just six seasons, an achievement that speaks volumes about his consistency and dedication. Ronaldo was instrumental in Real Madrid's dominance in Europe, contributing significantly to their four UEFA Champions League titles during his tenure (2014, 2016, 2017, and 2018).

His performances in Madrid were characterized by remarkable athleticism, tactical intelligence, and a hunger for goals. Ronaldo evolved his game to become more of a central striker, utilizing his aerial prowess, positional sense, and lethal finishing. His impact went beyond individual accolades; he was a leader on the pitch, driving his team to numerous victories and titles.

Legacy of Dedication and Excellence

Ronaldo's stints at Manchester United and Real Madrid are testament to his extraordinary work ethic and pursuit of excellence. He set new standards in professional football, not only in terms of skill and talent but also in terms of dedication and discipline. His relentless drive to improve, to adapt, and to succeed at the highest levels of football has inspired a generation of players.

Cristiano Ronaldo's sustained success at the pinnacle of world football is a reflection not only to his natural talent but more significantly to his unwavering commitment to training, fitness, and maintaining peak performance levels. Ronaldo's approach to his physical and mental preparation is as disciplined and methodical as it is extraordinary, setting him apart even among the elite athletes in the sport.

Training Regimen and Discipline

Ronaldo's training regimen is the cornerstone of his footballing longevity and success. He is known for his rigorous and meticulously planned workouts, both on and off the field. At the club level, Ronaldo often engages in additional training sessions beyond the team's regular practices, focusing on enhancing his strength, speed, and agility. His training regime includes a mix of high-intensity drills, technical skills work, cardiovascular exercises, and targeted strength training to improve his overall athleticism and footballing abilities.

His discipline extends to all aspects of his fitness regime. Ronaldo is known for his strict diet, which is carefully tailored to optimize his physical condition and performance levels. He pays close attention to his nutrition, hydration, and rest, understanding that these are as crucial to performance as the training itself. This holistic approach to fitness and wellness has been a key factor in his ability to perform at the highest level consistently.

Physical Attributes and Adaptation

One of the most striking aspects of Ronaldo's career has been his physical transformation and adaptation. He entered the professional football scene as a slender teenager with incredible agility and speed. Over the years, he has transformed his physique into that of a powerful athlete, capable of competing against the most robust defenders. This physical evolution is a direct result of his commitment to a rigorous fitness regime, focusing on building muscle strength, endurance, and explosive power.

Ronaldo's ability to adapt his style of play with his changing physical attributes is equally noteworthy. As he matured, he transitioned from a fleet-footed winger to a prolific striker, altering his game to maximize his efficiency and effectiveness on the field. This adaptability has extended his career and maintained his status as one of the best in the game, even as he navigated different phases of his physical peak.

Mental Strength and Professionalism

Ronaldo's approach to maintaining peak performance is not limited to physical training and nutrition; it also encompasses a strong mental attitude. His mental fortitude, focus, and professionalism are integral components of his success. Ronaldo approaches each training session, each game, and each season with a relentless desire to improve and succeed. His competitive nature drives him to push his limits continually.

His professionalism in managing his career is exemplary. Ronaldo is meticulous about his recovery processes, understanding the importance of rest and recuperation in a demanding sport like football. He utilizes a combination of rest, physiotherapy, and modern recovery technologies to stay in optimal shape.

Influence and Inspiration

Cristiano Ronaldo's commitment to maintaining peak performance has set a new benchmark in professional sports. He has redefined what it means to be a professional athlete in terms of preparation, training, and longevity. His example serves as an inspiration to aspiring athletes, illustrating that talent, while crucial, must be coupled with hard work, discipline, and a relentless pursuit of excellence.

Role Model and Legacy

Ronaldo as a Role Model

Ronaldo's journey from a humble background in Madeira to becoming one of the world's greatest footballers is a source of inspiration for many. He epitomizes the idea that with enough hard work and determination, one can overcome any obstacle and achieve their dreams. His dedication to training, fitness, and constant improvement makes him an ideal role model for young athletes in football and beyond.

His meticulous approach to his career - from diet and training to mental preparation and recovery - shows a level of professionalism and dedication that is rarely seen. Ronaldo does not rely solely on his natural talent; instead, he complements it with a rigorous work ethic. This message, that success is a result of hard work as much as talent, resonates with young athletes striving to reach the top of their sports.

Influence on Young Players

Ronaldo's influence extends beyond his fan base to impact young players across the globe. Many emerging footballers look up to him, not just for his skills and achievements on the field but for his discipline and attitude towards the game. His focus on continuous improvement, setting personal goals, and relentless drive to win has set a benchmark for aspiring footballers.

In training facilities and academies worldwide, Ronaldo's routines and training methods are often emulated. His impact is such that he has redefined what it means to be a professional athlete in terms of physical preparation and longevity in the sport.

Legacy in Football

Ronaldo's legacy in football is multi-dimensional. On the field, he will be remembered as one of the greatest ever, with numerous records, titles, and personal accolades. Off the field, his legacy will be defined by his professionalism, work ethic, and the way he has conducted his career.

Throughout his tenure in clubs like Manchester United, Real Madrid, and Juventus, Ronaldo has consistently pushed the boundaries of what is possible, both in terms of individual performance and team success. His influence in these clubs goes beyond the goals and the trophies; he has been a leader and a motivator, elevating the standards of those around him.

Ronaldo's Broader Impact

Beyond the realm of football, Ronaldo has become a cultural icon, known for his philanthropic efforts and his role as a global ambassador for various causes. His journey is a testament to the power of sports as a tool for positive change, both in an individual's life and in the broader community.

Cristiano Ronaldo's work ethic and career trajectory have made him a role model for millions around the world. His legacy in football will be remembered for his incredible achievements and for the exemplary determination and discipline he demonstrated throughout his career. Ronaldo has shown that while talent can get you far, it is hard work, dedication, and a constant pursuit of excellence that truly define a sporting legend. As aspiring athletes look to him for inspiration, Ronaldo's legacy continues to grow, influencing and shaping the future of football and sports in general.

References

Battista, Brianna. *Cristiano Ronaldo*. Rosen Publishing Group (2018)

Baxter, Kevin. *Soccer legend Mia Hamm's greatest win might be the debut of Angel City FC*. Los Angeles Times (2022). https://www.latimes.com/sports/soccer/story/2022-04-24/mia-hamm-angel-city. Accessed November 29, 2023

De Guzman, Chad. *How the Women's World Cup Evolved Into What It Is Today*. Time.com (2023). https://time.com/6289539/womens-world-cup-2023-history/. Accessed November 26, 2023

Murray, Scott. *A brief history of the Champions League – and why it's so hard to win two in a row*. The Guardian (2015). https://www.theguardian.com/football/2015/jun/03/champions-league-brief-history-barcelona-juventus. Accessed December 02, 2023

Perez, Mike. *Lionel Messi*. Welbeck Publishing Group Limited (2020).

Riner, Dax. *Pelé*. Lerner Publishing Group (2010)

Solo, Hope. *Solo: A Memoir of Hope*. HarperCollins (2013)

Staunton, Peter. *Mohamed Salah: The Prince of Egypt*. Goal.com (2018). https://www.goal.com/story/salah-egypt/index.html. Accessed November 20, 2023

Stead, Matt. *Ronaldinho: One of the greatest entertainers of all time*. Football365 (2020). https://www.football365.com/news/everybody-loves-ronaldinho-barcelona-brazil. Accessed November 30, 2023

Sudarshan, N. *Sunil Chhetri: The epitome of a modern-day footballer*. SportStar (2023). https://sportstar.thehindu.com/football/sunil-chhetri-feature-stats-records-indian-football-isl-bengaluru-fc/article67105192.ece. Accessed December 04, 2023

Bonus: Free Book!

Are you ready to delve into the thrilling book in the series, absolutely free? Get ready to go deep into the world of yet another football legend! Just use your smartphone or tablet to scan the QR code below, then follow the simple prompts to receive the PDF.